Coffee
with
Anthony

LIFE LESSONS FROM
ANTHONY TRIMBLE

◇

COMPILED & EDITED BY MICHAEL ENSEY
WRITTEN BY VARIOUS AUTHORS

dustjacket

Published by Dust Jacket Press
Coffee with Anthony: Life Lessons from Anthony Trimble/Compiled and Edited by Michael Ensey

ISBN: 978-1-953285-45-4

Dust Jacket Press
P.O. Box 721243
Oklahoma City, OK 73172

Ordering information for print editions:
Christian Life & Leadership Ministries
www.MichaelEnsey.com
info@michaelensey.com

All Scripture quotations not otherwise designated are from the King James Version of the Bible.

Permission to quote from the following copyrighted versions of the Bible is acknowledged with appreciation:

The Holy Bible, English Standard Version. ESV® Text Edition: 2016. Copyright © 2001 by Crossway Bibles, a publishing ministry of Good News Publishers.

Holy Bible, New International Version®, NIV® Copyright ©1973, 1978, 1984, 2011 by Biblica, Inc.® Used by permission. All rights reserved worldwide.

New King James Version®. Copyright © 1982 by Thomas Nelson. Used by permission. All rights reserved.

Holy Bible, New Living Translation, copyright © 1996, 2004, 2015 by Tyndale House Foundation. Used by permission of Tyndale House Publishers, Inc., Carol Stream, Illinois 60188. All rights reserved.

Permission from Weldon Music Publishing to quote lyrics from the following copyrighted songs is acknowledged with appreciation: "All I Am," "Come What May," "Dream of Heaven," "I'm Here to Worship," and "Like Our God."

Back cover photo credit: Colton Paul
Cover & interior design by D. E. West / ZAQ Designs - www.zaqdesigns.com
                    for Dust Jacket Creative Services

Printed in the United States of America

DEDICATION

To Kingston, Davis, and Graham

Your father was such a great man. He was a loving husband, a devoted father, a faithful son, a caring brother, a loyal friend, a visionary leader, an anointed singer, an inspirational songwriter, and a powerful preacher. Most important of all, he was a Christian. He loved you more than anything in this world, and we hope that through this book you will get to know him a little better.

◇

CONTENTS

SPECIAL NOTE

The authors are not personally profiting from this book. One hundred percent of this project's proceeds will be used to support missions and ministry, including a scholarship fund in Anthony Trimble's name. The proceeds will initially go toward a college fund for Anthony's boys.

───────◇───────

CONTRIBUTORS

Bradly DeLong

Michael Ensey

Chris Green

Jason Huckaby

Matthew Johnson

Stefani Nowacki

Jeremy Painter

Jason Staten

Anthony Trimble

Debra Trimble

Lysandra Trimble

Ryan Trimble

Thomas Trimble

Dustin Williams

───────◇───────

FOREWORD

Lysandra Trimble
Anthony's Wife

Anthony taught us how to live for Jesus in so many ways. But I will be forever changed by the remarkable way he also taught me how to die. Anthony ended his earthly life the very same way he lived day to day. Although he had little left in the end, he continued to pray over others, speak into people's futures, play one last game with his boys, and watch one more movie with his family and friends. When he reached the point at which he could no longer physically walk, his spirit walked in assurance, grace, and peace.

When we've lived out our years, it seems easier to say, "I have finished my course; I have kept the faith." But when our years are seemingly cut short and things feel left undone, it's a great sacrifice of praise to say, "Your will be done, Jesus." The few times Anthony said to me, "I have so much more to give, Soni," my whole heart agreed; I had believed he would do so much more. Time and time again I watched Anthony surrender his will with an honest and full heart. We fervently prayed and believed for healing until the very end, but at the close of every prayer there was total surrender.

The thing we both did not realize was that the Great Multiplier is at work even in times of great sorrow, tragedy, and death—as well as in the prayers that seem to go unanswered. He is orchestrating our lives even when we don't hear the music. Anthony's life on earth is still speaking and ministering to this generation. What seems like the end can be a catalyst for greater works. One day our flesh may fail, but we will not die. Our life will simply transition beyond this earthen vessel. All we have given and lived out will live beyond our flesh. Our only job is to stay close to Jesus and keep him at the helm. Trust Jesus in all things and at all times!

In closing I want to give a very special thank-you to the writers who have contributed special moments in time, thoughts about Anthony, and simply the feelings that emanate from these pages. I appreciate your time investment in this project, as well as the dear friendship each of you gave to Anthony. Thank you so much for loving our boys too!

———————◇———————

Thomas Trimble
Anthony's Dad

I remember when Anthony scheduled coffee with me. It frightened me because getting coffee was something he did with everyone else, not necessarily with me. We communicated throughout the day and the week. We talked lyrics sitting at the piano together, shared during staff meetings, or talked over a meal at the house. However, one of my favorite things Anthony did was the drop-in coffee visit. He would go to Starbucks early and get my favorite wet cappuccino with nonfat milk and stevia, and my wife's favorite pumpkin spice latté. Then he would surprise us by walking through the door on a random morning with a mischievous smile, yelling something ridiculous. We enjoyed that more than words can say. (When Lysandra did the coffee drop-in on the morning of my recent birthday, it was superb. Who else could do that? She is amazing! We visited over our favorite drinks for an hour and a half, and it was heaven.)

But when Anthony scheduled coffee one day, I knew that meant his health was declining more rapidly. It was difficult not to weep during our meeting at Picasso's, but I could see again the depth of his courage and the foundation of faith upon which he had built his life. Anthony loved to talk about ideas. He was never more animated than when playing with his children or discussing church growth and development. Anthony changed my approach to preaching. He worked for hours on his bottom line in a message. He preached with great passion and anointing. And I so enjoyed watching him develop from a child songwriter to an anointed psalmist.

I still have coffee with Anthony. There are days I go to his resting place, unfold a chair, and try to think of how he would improve the bottom line of a message I'm working on or the lyrics of a song I'm writing. He still inspires me every day. His humor, love of life, songs, voice, courage, and compassion and love for people still minister to me.

If Anthony's life and being were distilled down to one word, it would simply be this: *worshiper*. At the core. Whether he felt good leading worship at a conference or a service before his diagnosis, or whether he was bedridden with his last few breaths, he was a true worshiper. He worshiped through weakness, praised through problems, and sang in the rain. We wrote a song together just days before his promotion. Praise was always on his lips. I've seen him lift his hands in church when it cost him so much. He said, "It's all I can do." It was the widow's mite. He gave of his living. Would to God we would all follow his example. Anthony's life said, "I'm here to worship. I'm on this earth to bring glory to God." To quote his son Davis, "We were blessed."

This book is a tribute to Anthony's influence. His worship is still affecting his generation, and his courage is still being heard around the world. This book also includes writers who influenced Anthony. People like Michael Ensey took the time to encourage him when time was in short supply. One morning after Anthony's diagnosis, he contacted Michael to see if he could get coffee and talk. Although he was in the middle of his annual mid-winter youth ministries meeting, Michael said yes to an early coffee fellowship. Jason Huckaby was another constant confidant, mentor, and friend.

Thank you to his mentors and friends. You often spoke into Anthony and Lysandra's lives with anointing, clarity, and objectivity. And thank you to everyone for every prayer. Anthony's courage still speaks to me. The same faith that brought him victoriously through cancer is the same faith that inspires us to find victory in grief. Anthony lives on in every kind and courageous kingdom act.

Schedule coffee with someone and encourage him or her. Please pay it forward the way Anthony would, the way others helped him. And perhaps years from now your name will be in the title of a similar book.

Debra Trimble
Anthony's Mom

These are my thoughts of my firstborn, Anthony Bar Thomas Trimble. September 10, 1985, was one of the most joyous days of my life. It was the day God gave us our firstborn son. His name means "priceless," and he was and truly is priceless. What joy he brought us during his almost thirty-six years of life! In contrast, July 29, 2021, at 1:39 PM was the saddest day of my life. I journaled, "How will my heart ever quit hurting? How can I live life normally again?"

Anthony loved music from the time he could move around. As a toddler he would crawl to the piano, pull up to reach the keys, play notes with his fat little baby hands, and dance. I gave him wooden spoons and my pots and pans to simulate playing drums as I cooked in the kitchen. I recall singing praises and praying together with little Anthony and marching around our coffee table as if it were the walls of Jericho that were about to fall.

As a toddler he would be one of the first on his feet to praise, shouting, "Hallelujah!" as best as his little voice could say it. He began writing songs as a child. He was a worshiper of the King of kings. He wrote the song that says, "Shout it out, this is why I was made, to bring glory to your name."

Anthony taught us how to worship in the good and the bad times. At the end, it took so much out of him just to come to church. In one of his last services, as he made his way to the front of the church to worship, he told his wife, "This is all I can give." He could no longer preach passionately or lead anointed worship from the keyboard. It took every ounce of his strength to raise his hands and worship, but that's what he did. He was a modern-day psalmist, worshiping and glorifying God even during the hardest fight of his life. During his final hours I whispered in his ear, "Son, you're going home to be with Jesus soon. Find David and write some songs together." I also whispered to him, "Son, tell the Lord for me, 'Ain't no rock gonna take my place!'"

I miss the times when out of the blue and for no particular reason, he would show up at our home with flowers for his mom or with our favorite Starbucks drinks.

I'm so thankful he completed his race faithfully. As the scripture says, "I have no greater joy than to know my children walk in truth." Most often children lose their parents first in death. It was the greatest pain in the world to watch my child suffer and take his last breath on earth. But I'm blessed to know Anthony crossed the finish line and remained faithful to the end. In the final week of his life as we prayed around his bed, he lifted his arms in prayer and said, "God, your will be done," and he spoke in a beautiful heavenly language. That is the memory I treasure the most.

I will also treasure a moment spent with him a few weeks before he left his earthly body. Our family had taken one last short vacation very close to home. One morning I awoke early and looked out the window. Anthony was sitting alone by the pond. I hurriedly dressed so I could share some alone time with him. (He and I were always the early risers in the family.) As we sat overlooking the pond and chatting, we started worshiping and singing, "Tell me, Where is my help coming from? It's coming from the Lord; it's coming from the Lord!" Anthony paused, pointed his finger, and said, "You know, that's been my favorite song since NAYC 2019."

I have a child who is worshiping the "King of glory" in paradise, and I believe with all my heart that Anthony is fulfilling many of the songs he wrote and recorded. He is fulfilling his song that says, "I can't help myself, I can't help but worship at your feet." At Anthony's beautiful homegoing service on August 3, 2021, the closing song was one he wrote called "Dream of Heaven." This mother is looking forward to the day when we will be reunited. Until then, precious Anthony, I will "Dream of Heaven." Thank you for showing us how to live life to the fullest and worship through the pain.

ACKNOWLEDGMENTS

The finished product we call a book is never the work of just a single person. That is certainly true of this particular project. Any book worth reading requires an entire team of people who come together to make it the best it can possibly be before it is ready for public consumption. I am grateful for the tremendous team that helped make this book possible, many of whom I will acknowledge here.

Anthony, thank you for being you and for being my friend. Thank you for having coffee with me and for providing the inspiration for this book. Our hearts still ache. We love you and we miss you.

Lysandra, thank you for standing by your man and showing the world how to be a loving and supportive spouse during the most difficult and challenging trial of your life. You and Anthony were such an amazing team in every sphere of life, especially the most important—that of family and ministry. Thank you for the opportunity to write this book. We could not and would not have written it without your support, guidance, and feedback. The words you wrote in the foreword were beautiful and inspiring.

Tom and Debbie Trimble, thank you for raising Anthony to be the kind of godly young man whom others would look to as a Christian example and an inspiration of how to live life to the fullest. Thank you for sharing him with the world. We live in a better place because of Anthony. Thank you also for sharing from your heart the powerful words you wrote in the foreword.

Thank you to Anthony's siblings, Ryan and Stefani, for your contributions. Your unique perspective proved to be an invaluable element in the making of this book. No one but you will ever know the emotional currency required to bravely face your feelings and put your thoughts into written words.

Thank you to Anthony's friends and ministry peers who invested time, energy, and emotion into writing the chapters for this book. Anthony loved each of you, and it's obvious that you loved him too.

Thank you to my cousin Lori Green, who paid for the first copy of this book before I officially even started the project. You inspired me to write.

To Stan Gleason and Brian Kinsey, two of my favorite authors, thank you for sharing your expertise and experiences. Your guidance helped me immensely during this project, and your encouragement helped me to complete it. I am grateful for your friendship and support.

Thank you to my father, Randy Ensey, and my grandfather Jerry Ensey for reviewing the manuscript, offering feedback, and suggesting revisions. You are my spiritual heroes.

Thank you to my editors, Patricia Bollmann and Jonathan Wright. You made a good book great with your insight, creativity, and proficiency.

Thank you to my publisher, Adam Toler with Dust Jacket Publishing, for sharing your vast knowledge of writing and publishing books. It has been a pleasure to get to know you and work with you. I'm already looking forward to our next book.

Thank you to my family—my wife, Rebecca, and my amazing kids, Lincoln, Grant, and Avery—for giving me the grace and the space to manage this project. I love each of you more than words could ever say.

Thank you to my Lord and Savior, Jesus Christ. You are the reason that Anthony lived his life, and you are the reason we wrote this book. It is our prayer that people will see you and get to know you better through the life that Anthony lived.

And finally, thank you to everyone reading this book. I trust you will be encouraged, inspired, and challenged. May we all live a little more like Anthony.

—Michael Ensey

PREFACE

By **Michael Ensey**

The first time I met Anthony was the summer of 1989 in Orlando, Florida. We were at Disney World, and our families just happened to run into each other. I was eleven years old and he was not quite four. Our fathers had been friends for many years, and we spent a few moments together as our parents reminisced about old times. As an adult, Anthony took his own family to Disney World for several family vacations. He loved taking them to that magical place where dreams come true. Anthony was a visionary who was always dreaming of the next great thing into which he would pour his passion and creativity.

Years later our paths crossed again when he was in his late teens. He was traveling with his parents, ministering at youth camps and youth conventions. Some of those meetings were in Texas, where I was serving in youth ministry at the time. He was so anointed and talented that even at a young age it was obvious the hand of God was upon him. Our friendship began to develop. In fact, his family was ministering at our church in Conroe, Texas, the Sunday in 2004 when they were elected pastor of Restoration Church (formerly Winds of Pentecost) in St. Charles, Missouri.

In 2009 my family moved to St. Louis, Missouri, to work at the United Pentecostal Church International (UPCI) World

Headquarters, and the close proximity of our families enabled us to spend more time together. During this time Anthony began assisting the UPCI Youth Ministries with various projects, and the opportunity to work together strengthened our friendship. I have never met anyone with such a genuine heart for God and for people.

In November 2015 everything changed when Anthony was diagnosed with stage-four colon cancer. It seemed absolutely impossible. He was too young. Too healthy. Too important to his family. Too valuable to his church and the kingdom of God. Yet after the initial shock, Anthony faced this challenge the same way he faced every other challenge: with faith and determination. He knew it would be an important part of his life story, the ultimate testimony of the faithfulness and goodness of God. He was so right.

During this season of Anthony's journey, we began meeting almost weekly for coffee. It was a special time for me. I had a front-row seat to watch a man who was demonstrating incredible courage in the face of adversity. He never complained about his condition or symptoms; that was not his focus. Even when I knew he was in pain, there were no negative comments about his treatments and side effects. Instead, those special times of fellowship were always filled with hopes and dreams. He stayed focused on his purpose with a vision for the future. I was encouraged, challenged, and many times convicted. He would thank me every time we met, but I would try to convince him that I was the one who was the blessed recipient during those special coffee visits. I didn't realize at the time that the only reason he was wearing a suit and tie was for our coffee meeting. He would then go back home and shed the dress clothes in order to rest and recover.

One of our most memorable meetings was on Monday, June 12, 2017. The previous day I had preached for the very first time at Christian Life Center in Heath, Ohio, where I would eventually become pastor. After preaching at CLC that Sunday, my wife and I traveled back home to St. Louis. On Monday morning I woke up early and was in the kitchen preparing for my morning run. My mind drifted back to the previous day, and I began thinking about the possibility of becoming pastor of that church. They needed a pastor, and I was nearing the end of my term as UPCI General Youth President. It was then that God literally knocked me to the floor with this question: "Will you go?"

I don't think God was asking for my opinion. The answer was clear and obvious. I began praying the prayer of Moses found in Exodus 33: "If your presence will go with us, we will go" (my paraphrase). It was a powerful moment, that calling to Heath, Ohio, when I felt the weight of the pastoral calling. I woke my wife from a dead sleep. I think I scared her because she asked, "What are all the tears about?" I shared with her my experience and how God had spoken to me so clearly that we were to pastor CLC. The next person I shared that experience with was Anthony. It just so happened that our weekly scheduled coffee visit was that Monday morning.

We met at Picasso's Coffee House off of Fifth Street in St. Charles, Missouri. I still remember where we sat—the first table by the front door. I told him about the service the previous day—the church, the city, the people. I told him how God had called us that very morning to pastor that church.

He rejoiced with me. We laughed. We cried. We prayed. We dreamed. And we had coffee. It was what we always did.

In October 2017 our family moved to Ohio, but the distance did not diminish our friendship. We stayed in close contact. Every time I visited St. Louis for a meeting at the UPCI World Headquarters or to attend a class at Urshan Graduate School of Theology (UGST), we would manage to spend time together and drink some coffee.

The Lord kept Anthony and worked many miracles of healing, some of which you will read about later in this book. He was declared to be cancer-free during his almost six-year battle, but the cancer returned. He was mostly stable and strong until he contracted COVID-19 in March 2020. His weakened immune system was further damaged, and from that time on the cancer became very aggressive. But it was during this time that he preached some of his greatest sermons and wrote some of his most powerful songs.

It was also around this time that Anthony told me he was going to write a book titled *Coffee with Michael*. His inspiration was a book by Mitch Albom titled *Tuesdays with Morrie*. Morrie Schwartz had been one of Mitch Albom's college professors. Mitch rediscovered Morrie in the last months of the older man's life. Knowing he was dying, Morrie visited with Mitch in his study every Tuesday, just as they used to do during Mitch's college days. Their rekindled relationship turned into one final "class" with lessons on how to live. "The truth is, Mitch," Morrie said, "once you learn how to die, you learn how to live."[11]

---

11. Mitch Albom, *Tuesdays with Morrie* (New York: Doubleday, 1997), 82.

The next-to-the-last time we had coffee together was Friday, April 30, 2021. I was in town to graduate from UGST with a master's degree in theology. Anthony picked me up from my hotel and took me to his newest favorite coffee shop in Old St. Charles. We talked about the future. We dreamed and schemed just as we always did, but something was different. He didn't drink much coffee that day. He wasn't feeling good at all. Neither of us mentioned it, but we both knew he was nearing the end of his journey.

On our way back to my hotel he took me by the neighborhood lot where they had just broken ground. He was building a new home for Lysandra and his boys. He said, "I hope I get to spend at least one night in this house with my family." Emotions spilled over for both of us as we silently drove away. Unfortunately, he was not able to fulfill that wish.

The last time I had coffee with Anthony was ten days before he passed away. He had been asking if I would come preach at Restoration Church and spend some time with him. His father, Pastor Tom Trimble, called me and told me I had better come soon if I wanted to spend some quality time with Anthony. We stayed in a hotel close to the church so we could maximize our time together.

One afternoon during that visit, Anthony and I were alone in his hotel room. It was a tough conversation. He felt bad, almost guilty, because of his sickness. The world had celebrated his miracle of healing as he sang and testified at North American Youth Congress (NAYC) 2017, and he felt as though he had let them down because his cancer had returned. I assured him as best I could that his current condition did not diminish in any way his past miracle. Every person whom Jesus healed in the gospels—even those he raised from the dead—eventually experienced a physical death. There are still people to this day who are watching his NAYC testimony on YouTube and experiencing a miracle of healing because he inspired them to have faith in a God who heals.

He then began asking me some really hard questions. He asked if I remembered my dad, who had passed away when I was three and a half years old. I responded that I really didn't, but my first memory is from the day my dad died. Anthony asked me what it was like growing up without my biological father. He asked me how my mother managed. We talked. We cried. We prayed. He also apologized to me. "Michael, I'm so sorry I never got around to writing that book." I told him it was okay and that he didn't need to apologize—because I was going to write a book titled *Coffee with Anthony*.

I received one of the greatest honors of my life when Anthony asked me to speak at his Celebration of Life service. It was a life-changing day for me. On my way to the service, I stopped by Picasso's. Just me, my coffee, and thoughts of my friend. During the service I was inspired and challenged as every speaker shared his perspective of this incredibly humble yet gifted man of God. He even led worship at his own memorial service through the wonders of modern technology. We wept, we worshiped, and I shared the story of how this book concept came to be. We also learned that Anthony was quite the dancer. You can see for yourself on YouTube. Search: "Anthony Trimble Celebration of Life." Thank you, Ryan, for the exceptional family video presentation.

This book is the fulfillment of the pledge I made to my friend. If you knew him, the words on these pages will serve as a beautiful reminder of the impact he made in your life. If you didn't know him, it is my honor to introduce you to Anthony Trimble. I trust you will be blessed, inspired, challenged, and changed by the encounter. At the end of each chapter you will find a section titled "Live like Anthony." Each of these sections contains practical instructions that will enable you to put into practice the life lesson presented in that particular chapter.

Anthony not only taught us how to die; he also taught us how to live by walking through the valley of the shadow of death without fear. He walked through that valley with amazing grace and rock-solid faith. Anthony lived a purposeful life, squeezing every ounce of potential out of his almost thirty-six years. He gave his all, leaving nothing in reserve. I miss you, Anthony, and I can't wait to have coffee with you in heaven one day. Surely there will be coffee in heaven, right?

Just a few months before we completed the final manuscript copy for this book, Lysandra sent me an email saying she had found something I might want to include in this book. Anthony actually did start writing his book, and the words he wrote are the introduction you are about to read.

INTRODUCTION

By **Anthony Trimble**

Isolated. Alone. Have you ever been there? Are you there now? One of the worst scenarios in your valley and in your battle is to find yourself alone. Some people are introverts, as I was for most of my life. Some people are extroverts and thrive on being around others. Here's the bottom line: you need people around you to keep you from being isolated not only physically but also emotionally and spiritually, which is the greater danger.

The valley is the place where true friends are revealed. People will come out of the woodwork to tell you they are praying for you. They will say, "If you need anything, call me." But we all know the people who actually follow through with that invitation are few and far between. That is why it is so important right now to decide who your friends will be.

David had a table set for a feast in Psalm 23. Evidently it was in his valley because he wrote, "You prepare a table before me in the presence of my enemies" (Psalm 23:5 NKJV). My first question for you is not who your enemies are but rather who your friends are. Who is sitting at your table? If you could ask anything of anyone, whom would you choose? It is important that you take a good look at the people sitting at your table. You may need to make some changes—at least, that is how it was for me.

During my season of sickness a few friends called at least once a month to check on me. Good friends know your personality and how much time you need with them. Good friends know when to lie low and wait for the storm to blow over. Good friends are there right on time when you need them—not a week later. Some of my friends had very busy schedules, but they still found time to call.

So I have a few more questions for you: Do you have a friend you can laugh with through the valley? Do you have a friend who is a rock in your life? Do you have a friend who can pull you out of the darkness you're in? I guess the kind of person I'm talking about is not just a friend but more like a "big brother" or mentor—someone who can look you in the eye and tell you it's going to be okay when you need to hear it. Someone whom you respect so much that when he or she walks into the room, you stand a little straighter, almost as if a celebrity or important public official has walked into the room. Do you have that? I didn't at first.

The weeks following my initial diagnosis crawled by slowly. I created a cocoon of safety—a safe zone—and was very reluctant to come out of it. You've been there. You don't want to go to church because you're afraid of all the questions and all the "words of encouragement" you will get. I didn't want to focus on the valley. I wanted to walk right through it as if it never even happened. But eventually I had to get out of the ground-zero zone. Eventually I had to move forward and take another step. I knew I needed it, and I was looking for it.

It's easy to focus on the feeling in your stomach and the pain in your body when you have nowhere to go and no place to be. Every other week for ten months my mind was in a fog, and I needed something to get my mind off of the season I was in. A friend I admired and respected texted me one morning and asked if I needed anything. I replied, "Can we just go get coffee soon?" We set a time and place. Now, you have to understand that at this point I had been living in my pajamas for weeks. I had nothing to look forward to, unless you consider the snacks in the chemo room a highlight. I desperately needed some purpose in my life.

I knew my friend Michael Ensey had to dress in a suit and tie for work. Well, I wasn't going to be dressed in jeans and a T-shirt while having coffee with the UPCI General Youth President. I dressed in a suit and tie. For the first time in a long time I was dressed up and felt that I had somewhere to go and something important to do.

I rushed out the door and met Michael at a Starbucks close to his work. As we got settled at the table, the normal questions came out: "How are you doing?" "How is everything going?" "How are Lysandra and the kids doing?" But eventually we hit a rhythm. Michael wasn't just a great talker; he also was a great listener. I'm the type of guy who likes to keep making things better. I want to leave this world better than it was when I came into it. I want our church organization to have the greatest curriculum and music and videos this world has to offer. I knew Michael was one of those guys too. We talked about how to improve things. We talked about dreams and goals. We talked about vacation spots. We talked about his kids. We talked about my kids. It was definitely the kind of conversation you would have with an older brother.

This is what you need to be looking for in this "big brother" type of friend. This friend's number-one quality is that he or she doesn't affirm who you *are* but rather affirms who you *are becoming*. I can count four men in my life who have filled that role for me. Do you have someone like that?

I remember the day I received a call from someone who at that point had been only an acquaintance. I had admired and respected this person from a distance but had never really known him personally. This person phoned and asked if we could get lunch the day before he had meetings in town. We set a time and place to meet for lunch. What started out as "just lunch" turned into coffee and laughter and fellowship that fueled my spirit. This person became a friend I began to call on for counsel. He started to fill that "big brother" role in my life.

I remember another day as I was heading home from a chemo treatment. Another friend, someone I had looked up to for years, called and asked if he could see me. Before continuing, I'm going to let you in on what Mondays looked like for me. Every other Monday I had chemo treatment. I chose Mondays because if possible, I wanted to be better and feeling well enough to go to church by Sunday. I would come home from treatment and wait for the chaos in my body to begin. Tuesday mornings and afternoons were usually the worst. But *that* Monday I had a friend in my home, and we began talking about the things of the Lord. We talked about principles and virtues. I felt the Holy Ghost in the room. You need a friend like that. You need someone in your life to look up to, with whom you can talk about the things of God. You need someone that when he or she speaks, it stirs you and moves you.

On another occasion a friend came to the hospital during one of my treatments. I know I've already stated this, but I'm very leery about who is around me while I'm going through chemo. I don't want my kids to see me in that condition, let alone friends whom I respect and admire. However, I let this friend join me. He told me he would be there for only a short time and handed me a gift to keep me company while I was on this journey.

Two of these friends I just mentioned asked if they could meet me for breakfast one day at St. Louis Bread Company. When I walked in the door, I was surprised to find several additional friends there to present me with a gift. They had taken up donations for me at the UPCI World Headquarters and presented me with a money tree. I wish I could express to you how it made me feel that day. It drew me out of the darkness I was in. I felt special and loved.

If you know someone who is walking through the valley of the shadow of death right now, I challenge you to ask yourself how you can make that person feel special. Don't ask the person, "Is there anything you need?" Don't ask, "How are you doing?" Just *do something*. Find out what the person's favorite scriptural passage is. Find out what his or her favorite drink at Starbucks is. Find out what this person enjoys more than anything and figure out how you can bring it to him or her without having to be asked. Those are the greatest gifts—the ones that aren't asked for.

The greatest friends and family know the rhythm of the valley. They understand when to move in and when to move out. They know when to rush in like a protector and when to let you have some breathing room. Friends and family, you have a responsibility. You have a mandate during this season. You are to be the rod and the staff that comforts. You are called in this season to be an Aaron and Hur who strengthen the weary. God has placed you in that person's life for a purpose.

So pray about it. Ask God to give you wisdom concerning how to walk through this season with your friend. Ask God to give you wisdom in dealing with the future—not for you, but for your friend.

Job had friends, didn't he . . . ?

———————◇———————

PART ONE

Visions and Values

———————◇———————

Vision is the ability to plan the future with imagination and wisdom. A person with vision has the ability to see things that others cannot see or simply refuse to see. A value is a person's principles or standard of behavior; it is one's judgment of what is most important in life. Therefore, it is our vision that determines and guides our faith, and it is our values that motivate us to live out our faith so we can make the vision a reality. Anthony was a man of great vision and deeply held values.

Where there is no vision, the people perish:
but he that keepeth the law, happy is he.
(Proverbs 29:18)

For where your treasure is, there your heart will be also. . . .
But seek first the kingdom of God and
His righteousness, and all these things shall be added to you.
(Matthew 6:21, 33 NKJV)

———————◇———————

1

PRIORITY

The Value of a Well-Defined Life

———◇———

Dustin Williams
LIFE LESSON:
Anthony taught us the value of
a well-defined life.

The key is not to prioritize what's on your schedule
but to schedule your priorities.
—Stephen R. Covey

Organizational leadership responsibilities have a way of bleeding over into different areas of your life—time-consuming activities like calendar work, processing emails, and completing task lists. It takes deliberate action to keep those responsibilities from gnawing away at the time and attention that needs to be given to other important areas of life. My relationship with Anthony Trimble began in earnest on July 17, 2017, when we both were elected to serve our organization's district youth ministry. We had been entrusted with new roles and become fast friends as we plunged together into uncharted waters of leading conventions, youth camps, and ministry initiatives.

It was quickly evident to me that Anthony's life was already formed by a personal vision and values that pre-dated his election to serve the district. Over the course of many conversations and time spent working in close proximity, I observed in Anthony what I believe to be a key component of a life well lived. He had a remarkably clear and rigorously enforced definition of what was most important. His life was well defined.

I can remember the conversation at the campground that summer. For Anthony it was an afternoon coffee break. For me it was a soda break as I wasn't a coffee drinker. For this, Anthony hounded me constantly. Eventually I gave in and started trying sugar-filled coffee drinks. These were *not* coffee and likely were worse for my health than the sodas, but it appeased Anthony and served the purpose of opening up new caffeination possibilities for me.

Anyway, the conversation that day was not accidental—it was planned. We needed to talk. One year into our roles in district youth ministry, the spare time of our mornings, evenings, weekends, and vacations had been eroded by constant "this-or-that" needs relative to upcoming events that were in various stages of planning. Intervention was necessary.

We both had young families, and the primary ministry role for both of us was in our respective local churches. Thus, better and more clearly defined boundaries, priorities, and margin were needed. As we sat in a campground house that afternoon, Anthony made gentle suggestions that might help us (read "help me") get a better handle on containing the effects of district ministry in our personal and vocational lives. The result was a decision to have a scheduled weekly call to navigate urgent tasks, a practice our district youth department still carries on today. Call it containment. The conversation at camp that day imprinted me with the influence of Anthony's well-defined life.

BOUNDARIES

Boundaries are essential to success in one's personal arena of life. Genesis 1 records the creative work of God as he spoke oceans into existence. The writer of Job paints a picture for us of the moment when God said to the waters, "This far you may come, but no farther" (Job 38:11 NKJV). This simple act was the difference between chaos and order, between an out-of-control or a well-defined creation. It was necessary to ensure that everything else in God's creation was able to take place as planned. Much of what needed to occur on land could not happen if the waters were constantly infringing upon it. A great deal of the vegetation would not be able to withstand the salinity of ocean water. Entire geographical features would be eroded and lost forever if the waters were not given well-defined boundaries within which to reside.

So it is in life. It is very easy to allow the waters of vocational responsibilities to trespass into personal and family life. These waters seemed enormously important—vocation is a vast ocean full of unexplored possibility—but Anthony would not permit these waters to encroach on family time. His roles as a husband, father, and son were more important to him

than anything else—even the possibility or potential of anything else.

Understand this: you must establish boundaries and
develop a well-defined personal and family identity. It
takes saying "no" and "not right now" and requires you to
do so often. The tides of life's waters move and shift with
seasons, but there is a line they must never cross. This well-
defined dimension of personal and family life was at the
core of Anthony's identity. He excelled at other things in part
because he had this most important arena of life cordoned
off, defined, and set up for maximum investment.

Anthony's "vocational ocean" was broader and deeper
than most. Because of the strength of his inner life as
husband, father, and son, he was able to give himself fully
as a preacher, musician, songwriter, leader, and pastor. His
identity encompassed all of these areas and more because of
his Spirit-led and intentional boundary-defining discipline.

Your pursuit of a calling outside of the home is propelled
by the cultivation of your inner world. Author Gordon
MacDonald asked these penetrating questions: "Are we
going to order our inner worlds, our hearts, so that they will
radiate influence into the outer world? Or will we neglect
our private worlds and thus permit the outer influences to
shape us?"[11] Anthony was known for his anointed vocational
roles because of the dedication he demonstrated in his inner
world of private devotion, marriage, children, and family.
Vocational excellence does not happen by accident. It is
the result of guarding your inner life. It means sometimes
you have to say, "This far, and no farther." This is especially

---

11. Gordon MacDonald, *Ordering Your Private World* (Nashville: Thomas Nelson, 2003), 24.

important with regard to protecting time with the Lord and with family, which I witnessed Anthony do time after time.

The one time I saw Anthony become perturbed with someone was provoked by a passing innocent comment by someone who in some way placed Anthony's ministry as a musician above his ministry as a preacher. (Many other people made the same assumption, but his keen sense of God's definition for his life pushed back against that in his own kind and gentle way.) On the occasion I witnessed, Anthony caught himself quickly and recovered. He was every bit a minister of God's Word as he was a minister of music, and that's the way he walked in his vocation. He felt called as a preacher who also ministered as a musician, not the other way around. As we briefly discussed this in that moment, I caught a glimpse of a well-defined life that was growing in all directions, even if it wasn't immediately seen by everyone.

PRIORITIES

It comes as a surprise to no one that Anthony was not one-dimensional in his life or his priorities. The well-defined life is instrumental in protecting the various priorities you possess. It will lead you to richer personal identity. How many times in a month do you ask yourself, "How much of my time or energy is this going to consume?" This sort of evaluation is key to personal growth. A well-defined life is almost always one of thriving possibilities and admirable outcomes. I cannot count the number of times I saw Anthony turn down an opportunity in order to prioritize family. I'm referring not only to opportunities to go do something with public visibility. I'm including opportunities just to get a little more done during a day or a week. The temptation to churn out a bit more productivity is always present. It must never be allowed to overtake life's most important relationships and obligations. It's just not worth it. H. L. Hunt said, "Decide what you want; decide what you are willing to exchange for it. Establish your priorities and go to work."[12] It's the part about willingness to exchange that most encapsulates the point of this chapter.

"Let's put this on the list for Monday's call" is a phrase I must have heard Anthony say a hundred times. Like an endless game of whack-a-mole, seemingly urgent needs and tasks would emerge and seek to interrupt some other activity. It was one of Anthony's kind ways of saying, "No, let's not deal with this in all its complexity right now." He would say, "You know, let's put that in the notes for our next meeting." Of course, this was almost always the right thing to do, especially when the alternative was breaking up family time or interrupting weekly sermon preparation.

You can do this as well, and it does not have to be difficult every time you do it. As I mentioned earlier, his actions were the byproduct of that camp conversation in July 2017. You must set yourself up to be able to say no. Lest I have drifted into what may appear to be a fixation on the negative (that you must always say no), it deserves notice that we grow more in our "no" than we do in our "yes." This recognition is at the heart of a well-defined life. It is an orientation toward growth and fullness of identity.

---

12. H. L. Hunt, brainyquote.com/quotes/h_l_hunt_132394

Some things are worth protecting no matter what. Consider this your invitation into a conversation of priorities. Honestly evaluate how often you say yes to something without bringing it to the Lord in prayer, discussing it with a loved one, or processing it through your personal matrix of wise decision-making. I am not advocating for crippling trepidation—but rather conscious cultivation of peace and identity in a crowded, noisy, busy world.

MARGIN

Why go through the trouble of cultivating a well-defined life? If you cannot do it for yourself, do it for others. I never had to look to Anthony for his answer. All I had to do was look to his loved ones. The sort of definition I have presented in this space will be a blessing to others in your life. The kind of life that springs from these principles has the dual outcome of making you a healthier person and privileging the most important people in your life. All people aspire to have great relationships with the people closest to them. Those aspirations are realized in the sometimes-difficult moments of margin-guarding. Phillips Brooks wrote, "Character may be manifested in the great moments, but it is made in the small ones."[13] The health of your relationships will always correspond with the health of your personal margin.

The willingness to maintain appropriate margin is the underpinning force that empowers your ability to live out the example of Christ we find in Paul's letter to the church at Philippi. He instructs us to "look out not only for [your] own interests, but also for the interests of others" (Philippians 2:4

13. Phillips Brooks, goodreads.com/quotes/140794-character-may-be-manifested-in-the-great-moments-but-it

NKJV). "Others" includes not just the human beings in our lives but also God himself. We don't always think of God as someone we must deliberately include, but we know it is true that he does not push his way into a relationship with us.

Margin is the result of not allowing life to become overcrowded with the urgent or unnecessary. I have heard it said that margin is the space between your load and your limits. It is precious space, and it privileges one's relationship with Christ and those in your inner circle. Dietrich Bonhoeffer wrote, "We must be ready to allow ourselves to be interrupted by God. We must not assume that our schedule is our own to manage, but allow it to be arranged by God."[14] Margin is what allows divine interruptions to be blessings and not inconveniences. Margin is what keeps family time filled with joy instead of guilt, and it exists only in the presence of a well-defined life. Time with the Lord, family, and brothers and sisters in Christ creates depth of identity, personality, and vocation. Definition is what makes it possible.

CONCLUSION

Some lives stand apart because of how deeply they have impacted others. Anthony's life is a testimony of this. How can the effect of a life exceed the sum total of all its different parts? It is achieved in following Christ's example and organizing your life in a way that accomplishes the will of the Father in the lives of those around you. (See Philippians 2:5–11 for an extended vision of this in action.) There is no question that Anthony modeled his life in this way. The investment we make in others is in direct correlation to

14. Dietrich Bonhoeffer, *Life Together* (Minneapolis: Fortress Press, 2015), 76–77.

how submitted we are to the Christlike life in our personal, inner world.

I am happy to report that as of this writing I now drink one to two cups of black coffee each day. But that isn't the only way Anthony influenced my life. I often think of him and remember some of the lessons his life imprinted onto mine. So make this more than a chapter you read. Open up a conversation about life with a close friend of your own. Commit to one another that you will have honest dialogue about how you can each be spiritually healthy, intentional in your life patterns, and strong in investing in what matters most. Allow ongoing conversations like that to become imprinted into your life.

If the tasks, pace, and digital notifications of your life are overwhelming, take a lesson from my friend and do the work of clearing, defining, protecting, and maximizing. It is not best lived out as a knee-jerk reaction, although sometimes that feels like the only way to do it. Integrate it into the routines of life. Always remember to make things a matter of prayer. Consider "others" (Philippians 2:4). At first it may feel like mere containment, but stay the course. In time it will develop into contentment. The chaos will come to know its stopping point as the Spirit of Christ radiates from your inner life. Your personal identity will be richer because it will be formed in his likeness. And as a result of your Christlike looking after the "others" in your life, relationships will be healthier.

Some conversations call us to a deeper life. Below are several ideas to practically apply the ideal and principle of a well-defined life, to find everyday ways to live it out for God's glory.

LIVE LIKE ANTHONY

- Use the concepts of boundaries, priorities, and margin to create a well-defined focus for your life.

- Are you "present" no matter where you are? Don't allow your digital life to erode real-life interactions and moments. Be "fully there" by changing device settings (such as turning off notifications) and keeping the seemingly urgent from infringing into important time with the Lord and other people.

- Persistently protect time with loved ones. Schedule regular time with family, and do not interrupt it except for a true emergency. Maintain friendships and be proactive in setting up meetings for coffee or lunch.

- Experience the joy of living within structure and intentional priorities. Read a book that challenges you to write out life values and better organize your life around what matters most. And then do it!

- Organize your life in order to make maximum investment in what matters most. Become accountable to a close friend and initiate an ongoing, detailed, and honest conversation about spiritual disciplines, family time, and life goals.

2

PURPOSE

The Value of Personal Investment

—————◇—————

Jason Staten
LIFE LESSON:
Anthony taught us the value
of personal investment.

All growth is intentional.
To reach your full potential, you need a
sustained, intentional approach to
achieving all that God has in store for you.
You need both a purpose and purposefulness.
—Brian Kinsey

I had just finished preaching the final night of the Missouri District Holiday Youth Convention. I was wrestling with some of the thoughts and feelings that many preachers wrestle with after delivering a message. Had I effectively carried out the assignment God had given me? Did my preaching connect with the needs in the house? Were my words anointed and filled with compassion? These and other such questions always seem to be present with me, especially in the hours following such an occasion.

A few students were still lingering at the altars, and I was moving among them and praying for them when Anthony Trimble approached me. Until that moment I had not yet had the privilege of meeting him, though I was very aware of who he was. He was smiling and had a most cheerful disposition. He shook my hand, said a few kind words regarding the sermon, and then asked if it would be okay if he bought me coffee in the morning. He said he would meet me in the lobby at a certain time.

The next morning at exactly the stated time and in the stated place, there was Anthony with my caramel macchiato from Starbucks. For the next hour Anthony asked me various questions about ministry, family, and life in general. Although he wasn't taking notes, it was obvious he was eagerly storing away any information or advice that might be shared.

At the conclusion of our time together, Anthony asked if it would be okay to exchange numbers and stay in contact. I was honored first of all that he would care to hear what I had to say, and second, that he would have any desire to hear more. We exchanged numbers and thus began a friendship that would last until the time Anthony was called home.

Over the years since our first meeting for coffee, Anthony and I would meet up at conferences and conventions. He invited me to come and minister at Winds of Pentecost (now Restoration Church), and he came to minister at the church where I pastor. One of the things that really impressed me about Anthony is that he knew his purpose and was willing to invest in his personal growth. It was evident that Anthony Trimble was not going to sit back and watch life pass him by. He lived on purpose.

THE DESIRE TO GROW

There has never been a time in the history of humanity when there were more opportunities for personal growth. This statement is true across the spectrum of life, ranging from education and career, from the spiritual to the relational. Libraries of information are available at a few keystrokes on a laptop or a cell phone. Courses taught by experts in any given field can be downloaded and digested within a matter of moments. Software programs such as Logos bring an entire library of learning right to our fingertips. However, an inexhaustible library of information and unlimited opportunities for learning will produce few results in the absence of a clearly defined purpose and a hunger for growth. In contrast, the most meager accessibility to resources and limited opportunities cannot hinder the advancement of one with a burning desire for growth.

Benjamin Franklin was unable to receive formal education past ten years of age due to the family's financial condition. This did not stop Benjamin from learning and advancing in life. He would spend multiplied hours in the public library. Any money he was able to earn he would use to buy volumes of books. In spite of his lack of resources and limited opportunities, he achieved many great things, namely, his inventions of the lightning rod and bifocals as well as becoming one of the founding fathers of the United

States of America.[15] As the old saying goes, "Where there's a will, there's a way." When there is a hunger to grow, there will be growth.

The question might be posed, "How does one acquire the desire for growth?" I'm proposing a few simple answers to this question: First and foremost, a desire to grow will be determined by where you place yourself. It is obvious that plants grow in a garden. Similarly, if you want to grow, surround yourself with others who desire to grow. A plant in a garden does not grow in isolation; it grows in accordance with the others around it. Thus, it will be difficult to nurture a desire to grow if you are surrounded by others who are satisfied with their present condition. Anthony embodied this principle of growth.

Perhaps our conversations while drinking coffee were not so much about him gathering great advice but more about him recognizing my hunger to grow. In fact, I believed that my having coffee with Anthony was an occasion that was unique to me. Since his passing I have learned that I was just one of many who were having coffee with Anthony. He was intentional about placing himself in a garden surrounded by others who had a desire to grow.

Second, a desire to grow will be determined by whether or not you actually plant yourself. The sort of desire that brings about true growth is not a fleeting emotion or trend; it is a lifelong commitment. It is a devotion that outlasts the seasons and rises above the storms. You must plant yourself in the garden if you want to nurture a desire for growth. Again, Anthony demonstrated this commitment. In spite of sick-

15. Benjamin Franklin, *The Autobiography of Benjamin Franklin* (New York: Henry Holt & Company, 1916), 2–3.

ness and devastating prognosis, he never lost his desire to grow. I challenge you to plant yourself in a garden. Surround yourself with others who refuse to settle for the status quo. Make a determined commitment never to stop growing!

WILLING TO INVEST

Long before geofencing, the modern advancements of marketing corporations and advertisement departments learned just how much humanity likes the word *free*. Bold, highlighted phrases like *Buy one, get one free* or *20% more free* plastered strategically on products and packaging were proven to increase customer attraction. The fact is that we humans love *free*! But while we all appreciate *free*, there are legitimate drawbacks to being a freeloader.

First of all, we don't place much value on something that is provided for free. But we would greatly value the same resource if we had to invest our time or hard-earned finances in order to acquire it. When we invest, we have "skin in the game." Though it might seem to be a simple cup of coffee that Anthony offered to purchase, it was much more than the few dollars invested; it was the sixty minutes he could have been somewhere else doing something much more rewarding. He never allowed me to pay for coffee when we met (outside of the occasion he was ministering in the church that I pastor). He always ensured that he was the one paying for coffee. I believe a large part of that was his desire to put "skin in the game"—to make sure he had a vested interest in leaving the table with some nugget of knowledge or some added perspective.

In addition to this first benefit of being willing to invest, Anthony's persistence in paying for our coffee demonstrated the kind of character Anthony had. He was demonstrating his appreciation for my time. I would have had no problem paying for my own coffee and would have actually preferred to pick up the tab. However, the consistent insistence to cover the cost demonstrated to me an appreciation for what I might bring to the table. The impact this had on me was that I wanted to make sure that I gave him my best. I wasn't just passing time; I was sharing knowledge, experience, and understanding. The truth is that most of those times I met with Anthony, I walked away feeling as if I had gained more than I had given.

I once had a mentor tell me that when you give people something of value for free, you're robbing them of the opportunity to grow. I can state from personal experience that my capacity to grow is in direct proportion to my willingness to invest. When I am no longer willing to sacrifice, I am no longer able to grow. One of the inspirational podcasts that I listen to recommended that we appropriate 10 percent of our income toward investing in our growth. This obviously would be outside of our tithe into the kingdom of God. While I am not suggesting a certain percentage, I am suggesting there must be a tangible willingness to invest if you are going to fulfill your purpose.

INVEST TO ADVANCE

The desire to grow is a relatively rare quality. Many are simply looking to find a comfortable place where they can settle and live out an existence. They are not interested in investing. They live their lives floating from freebie to freebie, looking for bargain deals and loopholes that help them circumvent any sort of cost. These individuals leave behind little to no impact. And then there are those who row upstream, laboring against the current. They resist the gravitational pull of average and ordinary. They possess both the hunger to grow and the willingness to invest. They are advancing toward their purpose.

The Bible is filled with such examples; for instance, men like Abraham, a man who could have settled and lived comfortably in Ur but spent his life searching for a city whose builder and maker was God. Abraham invested in this passionate pursuit of God when he left a place that was familiar. He consistently built altars, offering sacrifices unto God, and was even willing to place his own son on the altar. Then there was Ruth, who could have remained in Moab and lived the life that had been passed down to her by inheritance. Yet she clave to Naomi and declared, "Wherever you go, I will go; And wherever you lodge, I will lodge; Your people shall be my people, And your God, my God" (Ruth 1:16 NKJV). Much like Abraham, she left behind a life of comfort and certainty and followed Naomi to Bethlehem. Here she toiled daily in the fields to glean remnants of grain that had been left behind by the harvesters. She was finally noticed by Boaz and became one of only five women named in Scripture in the lineage of Jesus.

The list of names that could be shared is nearly limitless. However, Jesus Christ is the ultimate example of someone having a clearly defined purpose that was expressed through this duality of a hunger to grow and a willingness to invest. "Jesus increased in wisdom and stature, and in favor with God and men" (Luke 2:52 NKJV). The hunger of Jesus to grow into his full potential was present in every aspect of his life and ministry. He showed that he was willing to invest and to pay the ultimate price to fulfill his purpose when he laid down his life. "Who for the joy that was set before Him endured the cross, despising the shame" (Hebrews 12:2 NKJV). The result? Thirty-three and a half years on this earth, and time itself was forever changed. Two thousand years later, the life of Jesus Christ is still the greatest story ever to be told, and lives are still being eternally changed. This is the outcome of lives that possess a laser-like focus on their purpose. None will ever rise to the level of impact that Jesus's life did, but many will advance his impact.

CONCLUSION

All who were close to Anthony would love to have experienced a few more years of his contagious laughter and another decade or two of his powerful songwriting and worship-leading. The truth is that we all feel that Anthony left us way too soon. However, in just thirty-five years he left us with an eternal imprint. He left this world having demonstrated that when there is the intersection of both a hunger to grow and a willingness to invest, the result is fulfilled purpose and a legacy that will never be forgotten.

LIVE LIKE ANTHONY

- Seek the Lord and study his Word to discover your personal purpose.

- List the top three areas relative to your purpose in which you need to grow.

- What are you currently doing to invest in your growth?

- What are you planning to start doing to invest in your growth?

———————◇———————

3

PURITY

The Value of a Pure Heart

———◇———

Chris Green
LIFE LESSON:
Anthony taught us the value of a pure heart.

You must keep all earthly treasures out of your heart,
and let Christ be your treasure, and let Him have your heart.
—Charles Spurgeon

"Read anything good lately?" Anthony asked in a text message just two months before he passed. Knowing that his time was limited, he pressed for more and continued to better himself. If he could not improve his physical body, he would better the things he could still control: his mind and his spirit. We traded book ideas about church growth and ministry. He explained, "When I die I don't want to leave behind any potential."

PURE WORSHIP

Eleven years earlier I walked into Winds of Pentecost for the first time. I had just moved from Austin, Texas, to St. Louis, Missouri, to attend Urshan Graduate School of Theology. Anthony's dad, Tom Trimble, was one of my classmates, and he invited me to visit their church. Unbeknownst to me, he was the pastor. The church building was quaint and unassuming with hardly an empty seat. Not knowing anyone there, I nervously made my way down the steep, narrow staircase leading into the basement level containing the classrooms. Sunday school classes were about to begin.

Unfamiliar to the customs of this church, I followed the crowd of young people into a common area, found a seat, and waited patiently for the Bible study to begin. Anthony walked into the room with a guitar hanging from his shoulder. He took his place front and center and began to sing "Healer," by Kari Jobe. As he sang about God being his healer, his portion, and his everything, for whom nothing is impossible, I knew instantly that Anthony was different.

The atmosphere changed as the Spirit of God filled the room. Everyone stood with hands lifted and voices raised as we worshiped the Lord, being overwhelmed by his presence. I remember thinking that this was a different way of doing Sunday school. Eyes full of tears, I knew God was in that room, and the young man singing was very much responsible for his being there. Anthony did not just sing—he *worshiped*. And when he worshiped, all of heaven heard his voice not because of the volume but because of the *purity*. I thought, *If this is how they begin their Sunday school class, I can't imagine what the church service is going to be like.* Before the church service had concluded that day, I knew this church would be my new home.

It did not take very long for Anthony and me to become friends. He and his wife, Lysandra ("Soni"), treated me like a brother. Four years later while giving a speech at my graduation ceremony, I expressed how God had not sent me to St. Louis to earn a master's degree from UGST; rather, God had sent me there to meet the Trimble family.

I was privileged to join the worship team for the church, playing the drums alongside Anthony as he led worship from the piano. We worked closely together as I interned for Pastor Tom Trimble. Back then, Anthony was often asked to lead worship for different church events, and he was kind enough to take me with him to play the drums. My heart longs to go back to those moments so I could better appreciate and recognize what I was witnessing in Anthony's presence. No matter the context or setting of the event, Anthony led worship with everything he had. I never saw him give less than all of himself in worshiping his Savior and compelling everyone around him to do the same.

For example, he once was tasked with leading a worship set at a small coffee shop full of all sorts of people—both believers and unbelievers. Where most Christians would have acquiesced and given a watered-down version of their ministry, Anthony worshiped as if he were leading a mass choir in front of thousands of saints.

25

PURE MOTIVES

Anthony possessed and portrayed the most unique ability to make you forget about everything going on around you. To Anthony traditions did not matter, the schedule did not matter, and ensuring that we got through all the rehearsed songs did not matter. The only thing that mattered was being completely immersed in the presence of God. Uniquely enough, his whole life was that way. That was his motive for everything he did.

Yes, he could be fun and goofy, but in every setting he maintained a purity and God-consciousness about him. Many words can be used to describe my friend, but if I had to choose one, I would say *purity*. There was always a purity about his spirit. Anthony would often tell me, "Chris, I want to see God move more than I have ever seen before. I want to see *real* miracles in my ministry." I would rebut by asking if he realized what happened when he was singing, worshiping, and preaching. "Anthony, you change the atmosphere every time you lead. There *are* real miracles happening in your ministry. You may not be healing every disease and emptying every wheelchair, but you bring people to God who thought they could never know him. When you lead worship, people get out of their seats of self-doubt and approach the altar as if they can't resist the compelling draw of God's love. They find themselves in the presence of God."

Looking back on Anthony's life and ministry, I have realized that his indelible impact on a service and on people was simply because of his purity. Jesus said, "Blessed are the pure in heart, for they shall see God" (Matthew 5:8 NKJV). He did not promise that the pure in heart would see notable miracles of healing or mass outpourings of the Holy Ghost—but rather they would simply see God. Is that not the greatest miracle—to see God?

This blessing is not only for the individual with a pure heart but also for those who happen to be in their presence. I have heard Pastor Tom Trimble preach many times that our lives and our ministry are not about reflecting ourselves but reflecting the image of God. Anthony's life reflected the image of God.

Death is a mystery we cannot fully understand, much less appreciate while on this side of eternity. Even when someone has lived a full life and dies at a ripe old age surrounded by family and friends, the death still leaves a void of grief and loneliness. This void is deeper when death makes an early arrival for such a friend as Anthony. God said of himself that he is a jealous God. I believe there are people who please God in such a way that it brings them to their reward sooner than most. The Bible says that before the translation of Enoch, he had this testimony, that he pleased God (see Hebrews 11:5). Anthony never lived to impress man but rather to wholeheartedly please his God. He had pure motives. What a testimony!

PURE POTENTIAL

From his diagnosis to his death, Anthony never asked the unanswerable question *Why?* Instead, we all watched as he used his condition to please God and bless the church. In those six years of pain, sickness, chemotherapy, and sleepless nights, Anthony wrote his best songs, preached his greatest sermons, and prayed his deepest prayers. That is why he could be lying in a hospital room on his twelfth round of chemo and send me a text asking, "Read any good books lately?" As stated earlier, the last thing Anthony wanted to leave behind on this earth was potential.

I had the privilege to preach at his church the Sunday before his death. He was far too weak to be there in person, but he still made his presence known while watching online from his home.

Anyone who knows Pastor Tom Trimble understands that punctuality is not one of his greatest strengths; he would rather finish a conversation with a friend than cut it short to arrive on time for service. That is what endears him to so many.

We were sitting together in Pastor Trimble's office shooting the breeze, not realizing that while we lingered the service start time had come and gone. Unsurprisingly, a text message came in saying, "Dad, why hasn't church started yet?" It was Anthony. We snapped to attention like soldiers to their general and hustled down to the sanctuary to begin the service. Anthony was neither content nor complacent even when he had every excuse to be.

After the service we were able to go visit Anthony and Soni in their home. I was grateful and yet nervous to see my friend in this condition, knowing it would likely be my last chance to visit with him. He was weak and in pain, but he sat in his recliner, blanket pulled up to his chest, eager to discuss the church service. To my amusement I watched him go through every detail with his dad, complimenting certain things and detailing ideas for improvement (beginning with a prompt start time). With only a few days to live, he was thinking not about himself but about his church. No potential left behind.

As Jesus hung on a cross minutes away from eternity, his thoughts, his words, and his prayer were not for himself but for the thief hanging beside him and for the soldiers responsible for his pain. Likewise, there was not a critical bone in Anthony's body—just an unquenchable fire to be better, better as a husband, a father, a friend, and a spiritual leader to so many. Great leaders like Anthony do not just pursue self-improvement; they also make everyone around them better. If there was room for growth, Anthony would find it and formulate the plan for improvement.

CONCLUSION

That Sunday afternoon in his home after a long talk about the things of God and sharing fond memories, we spontaneously began praying. The presence of the Lord swept into that living room. As we cried and praised God, a peace came over us and there was a holy hush. I was surprised when Anthony stood up on his own for the first time in many days, walked into the next room, and sat down at the piano to sing and worship God.

It was a new song that he and his dad were in the middle of writing together. As I sat and listened, tears filled my eyes and I was transported back to that first Sunday school class in the basement where Anthony's worship filled the room, making space for God's presence to abide. No one moved for over ten minutes as Anthony and his mother and father sang together. It was a holy moment. I hugged him for the last time, and just before I walked out of the house, he told me, "Chris, when I get to heaven I will watch after Sancy." Sancy is our daughter who died in 2020 at sixteen days of age. His purity to show his love for me in his condition is something I will never forget.

If I learned anything from Anthony's life, it was that a pure heart is a relentless love for God and for others. A purer heart cannot be found than that of Anthony Trimble. Yes indeed, "Blessed are the pure in heart, for they shall see God." Anthony, my friend, you are blessed, and now you are with the one you were longing to see.

LIVE LIKE ANTHONY

- What does it mean to you to have a pure heart?

- What are some practical ways you can pursue having a pure heart?

- Examine your heart and consider the purity of your worship, your motives, and your potential.

- What does "realized potential" look like in your life?

4

PROGRESS

The Value of Optimal Behavior

———◇———

Ryan Trimble
LIFE LESSON:
Anthony taught us the value of optimal behavior.

Progress means getting nearer to
the place you want to be.
—C. S. Lewis

Author Ray Bradbury once said of his friend Walt Disney that despite popular opinion Walt wasn't an optimist. He didn't simply think happy thoughts and expect a good outcome. Disney was what Bradbury called an "optimal behaviorist," which means, no matter the circumstance, Walt could muster whatever behavior was needed for progress. He behaved optimally.[16]

Anthony, my brother, was a man of good character prior to his diagnosis. However, some of my favorite life-lessons,

16. Ray Bradbury, "Ray Bradbury Talks about Knowing Walt Disney," Disney Avenue, interview by Leonard Maltin, youtube.com/watch?v=qknLq3NPgFo

the meat and potatoes, really come after his diagnosis, because of how he chose to meet his health challenges. He had already laid the groundwork of his character, his values. The sickness only revealed to a greater extent what kind of person he already was. And his response was optimal.

EARLY BIRD

He awakened early in the morning. As a teenager, he was up with the sun and down in the basement, recording and producing music. Even after he was married and had children, he enjoyed waking early and having his quiet time, setting his intention for the day without interruption. This was the time of day he seemed most inspired and energized.

We used to have early morning text competitions to see who would message the other first (usually it was a silly GIF). Who would be the first to wake, first to get going? It was fun. We enjoyed challenging and inspiring each other. It was also a way of feeling connected after I moved to Texas with my wife and kids. It was nice to know that he was praying while I was praying, that we were enjoying our morning coffee at the same time.

When he was healthier, he'd go work at his church office and knock out several important tasks before noon. This energized him like nothing else. I asked him once, if he could wave a magic wand and do music full time or church work (like a pastoral or administrative role), what he would choose. He said church work. It's interesting: after all the transcendent music he made, and with all his artistic sensibilities, he felt a clear call to church administration and pulpit ministry.

Anthony built relationships with church leaders and volunteers. He enjoyed the behind-the-scenes work of putting on a successful event or service. He'd grin from ear to ear when he'd see the work pay off, when a great idea would come to fruition, when a banquet or a Christmas program would go well. It brought him great joy to labor with his brothers and sisters in the Kingdom of God.

RESPONDING TO SICKNESS

After the 2015 diagnosis, he really got to work. He didn't curl up in a shell. He became more giving, more gracious, more compassionate. He counted the cost, as Scripture instructs, did the math, figured how many "good" weeks he'd have between treatments and calendared accordingly. He took Lysandra and the boys on several marvelous vacations (family was first), recorded over twenty five songs, released several singles, dropped three full albums, and left many demos and song-sketches. After we suspected Anthony's treatments would make pregnancy impossible, Lysandra miraculously gave birth to another son, Graham. Anthony worked on ideas to strengthen the church, improve systems, and audio/visual elements of the live services. He was the guy at midnight, up at the church, troubleshooting tech issues with the sound team.

Could he have kicked back, eaten ice cream, and binge-watched a thousand shows instead? Yes. And no one would have blamed him. But Anthony kept himself accountable to a high standard. He didn't throw a pity party. He learned what he was capable of between treatments, and he knew in his heart of hearts whether he was giving his all, to the best of his ability. Sometimes his "all" was simply to stand at church with his hands in the air and show us how to suffer well.

While he became known for his music, his pulpit ministry, and his journey with sickness, he seemed most concerned with his reputation in his own household. He told me once, "If the whole world admires me, but my wife and children have no respect for me, then I have failed."

A THIRST FOR GROWTH

Although he was a great guy, Anthony wasn't perfect. He wasn't super-human. He had areas, as we all do, that he was working on. But it was his willingness to get up every day and make progress—that's what was so admirable. Progress on himself, on his marriage, with his boys, progress in the church, progress on personal and professional projects. He liked getting up and getting things done. Pre-diagnosis, you could see him often at Starbucks in the morning on his laptop, working on a sermon. But after several years of treatments, surgeries, and setbacks, getting out and working at a coffee shop became a luxury.

Less than a year before his passing, he sent me a selfie one day. In the photo, he's sitting at a counter, near a cafe window, with his laptop open. I zoomed into the photo to see if I could make out what he was working on. Though it was blurry, I could see on the screen a Google form—a questionnaire, likely for church volunteers. I can imagine the form included things like *How can we be better? How can we help you? Share a challenge. Share a win. Share a goal.* In the photo he's grinning not just with his mouth but also with his eyes.

WHAT REMAINS

At the time of my writing this, it's been only a year since Anthony passed. At first there's the frantic obsession with preserving every photo, video, voice message, text, and crumb. You try to hold on to fragments of him, fragments of fragments—anything that will keep him a little more alive in your memory. Fragrances too (I still smell him on a couple of shirts I've kept. But that won't last much longer). When the dust settles, when the grains of sand slip through our fingers, we really have just a few lasting impressions of a person.

What endures, for me anyway, is that word—that one wonderful word *progress*. Call it *sanctification* if you like (that's its real name). But that's the idea! The appetite to seize the day. To be a better man. A thirst to learn something new. The courage to meet the mundane with enthusiasm and wonder. To put aside pain and make a moment magical for your kids. To see something through when others retreat. To choose a smile where others frown. Those are the things that stick with me.

CAROUSEL OF PROGRESS

Before the post-COVID-19 Disney controversies, Anthony and I talked a lot about the company and the brand. Our appreciation for Disney was not about the current leadership and direction of the company, but more about the founder, Walt, his values, work ethic, and lasting legacy.

There's an old Disney ride, dating back to 1964, called "Carousel of Progress." You sit in a moving auditorium and watch the American family evolve from the turn of the twentieth century to modern day. As technology changes and we see more conveniences and luxuries in the home, the animatronic characters sing the song "There's a Great Big Beautiful Tomorrow." I've always liked the song and the history of it, those ideas of mid-century optimism and industry.

Cut to August of 2020. I got a package in the mail with Anthony's home address on it. I tore open the seal and cut through the bubble wrap to find a colorful desk plaque. Anthony and his family had obviously just returned from a Disney trip and he'd gotten me a gift. The vibrant desk plaque, with gold trim (which sits on my desk as I write now) displays the words: *There's a Great, Big, Beautiful Tomorrow.*

Those words pretty much sum up his outlook. Each day is full of opportunity and we choose how we meet it: either with distain or with zeal, with a frown or smile.

CONCLUSION

Anthony ran his race well. He fought the good fight and endured for the joy that was set before him. And after he breathed his last breath, and we all wept and worshiped a good while, and the room became quiet and dark and still, Kingston, Anthony's firstborn, said, "Look! Dad's smiling!"

LIVE LIKE ANTHONY

- What does optimal behavior look like in your life?

- Decide how you want to be remembered before tragedy comes. Write your own epitaph and live in such a way that it comes true.

- Have something exciting to wake up for each day and set your intention for that day before it gets noisy.

- Make a commitment to value your private reputation more than your public reputation.

- Decide to make progress every day, even if it's just one small step.

———◇———

PART TWO

Relational Investment

One of the most important human capabilities that so often determines personal capacity is the ability to establish, develop, and maintain healthy relationships with the right people. These kinds of relationships require a lot of time and effort. Anthony understood this, and he was a master at genuinely making everyone in his world of influence feel loved and valued.

Don't just pretend to love others.
Really love them. Hate what is wrong.
Hold tightly to what is good.
Love each other with genuine affection,
and take delight in honoring each other.
(Romans 12:9–10 NLT)

Love is patient and kind. Love is not jealous
or boastful or proud or rude. It does not demand its
own way. It is not irritable, and it keeps no record of
being wronged. It does not rejoice about injustice

but rejoices whenever the truth wins out.
Love never gives up, never loses faith, is always hopeful,
and endures through every circumstance.
(1 Corinthians 13:4–7 NLT)

———————◇———————

5

LOVE

How to Value People

———◇———

Stefani Nowacki
LIFE LESSON:
Anthony taught us how to value people.

Life moves at the speed of relationships.
—Anonymous

It isn't easy telling someone you love goodbye for the last time. Your heart beats fast as the reality sets in that you will never see the person again on this side of heaven or hear the person's laughter or see his or her smiles. You pray and hope you can cling to and remember all the memories that seem so delicate now.

It took me over a year to truly feel able to write about Anthony, my brother. That's what I called him when we talked. His warm smile and loving nature were a constant encouragement that made me feel valued. He was there since the day of my birth, protecting and guiding me in the way big brothers do, always making time for me. That's what I loved about him.

HE LOVED ME

Anthony was a worshiper, minister, and psalmist to so many others, but to me he was my brother and my friend. I watched Anthony during his six-year battle with cancer as he faced each challenge head-on with purpose and intentionality. Once the chemo schedule was set for every other week, he strategically planned time for work, his family, others, and his dreams. "What you pursue reveals your priorities," Anthony would say. That was true of his life. Anyone could look at his schedule and know what he valued—his church, his family, and people. He was always leading with love. That was my brother.

On a sunny summer day in May 2016 Anthony called me and said, "Hey, Stef—my family is out of town for a few days. Would you like to have some brother-sister time?" He didn't have to say another word. I was all in. It was his off week of chemo, and we had the time of our lives for the next few days. We watched movies and ate way too many gummy bears. We splurged at Six Flags and Sky Zone. He even made time for a few brother-sister coffee dates. It was the ultimate week.

One night as we sat and talked, he took out my rarely touched beginner's guitar in the front room of Mom and Dad's house and asked if he could write a song with me. We went through the lyrics and different melodies until they all fit together like a puzzle. The chorus ended with the line "When smiles turn to tears, still after all these years you've always been around." Looking back at those memories, I smile through the grief of losing him. That chorus says everything I feel. He was always there for me—my brother.

HE LOVED OTHERS

But I wasn't the only one in whom he invested. Anthony had a way of loving people so genuinely. He valued relationships—those he could pour into and those from whom he could glean. Church days were his days to invest in others. While many came to church to take, he came to church to give. You would usually find him after service sitting and eating with different individuals in the church who needed encouragement or just fellowship.

Anthony loved as Christ instructed us: "Just as I have loved you, you also are to love one another" (John 13:34 ESV). His love for people was a genuine Christlike love. He had a way of investing in others, going above and beyond what most do. If someone was coming to paint the church, he was showing up with pizza. If someone was watching the kids, he was stopping by with a "thank you" latte. He always found ways to say, "I value your time and your sacrifice," not only through his words but also through his actions. And he genuinely did value them.

Just weeks before his passing, many of his friends and family came by to talk to him. He was too weak to do much, but he would reach out to lay his hand on his friends' shoulders and pray blessings over their lives and their futures. Even at the end of his life he was still showing love and investing in others.

A REMINDER FROM A LEAF

In the fall of 2015, when Anthony was first diagnosed with cancer, we were at a loss as to what his diagnosis meant moving forward. Questions and worries filled my mind as I drove toward my parents' home through the wet streets. As I walked toward the front door, a sea of bright yellows, oranges, burgundies, and reds captured my attention. It's strange how the things that seem so insignificant in day-to-day living have a way of speaking to us when we need it the most. I picked up a single leaf and held it in my hand. How extraordinary it was! Life was leaving it, and yet it was more beautiful than ever.

I now understood the song my dad had written many years ago that said, "I see the colors in the rain." Even among the tragedy of life there is still beauty and purpose. If God thought enough about this leaf to give it brilliant color and purpose as it was making its exit, how much more would he do that for his children? I was reminded of God's promises for us that day. God had not forgotten us. Even now, after the loss of our Anthony, God still has not forgotten us.

I held on to that leaf, and it now has a home in my journal. It remains a reminder that God is still sovereign through the autumns and winters of our lives. And as a leaf changes with the season, Anthony was more radiant at the end. He must have a beautiful mansion because he laid up all his treasures in heaven. His legacy lives on in the investments he made and the lives he loved.

CONCLUSION

I conclude with this prayer for all of us:

God, help us to love others as you have loved us.
Please help us to be your hands and feet. Open our eyes
to see those around us who need to be loved and need us to
pour into them. Please help us to be intentional about our
relationships. We want to invest in your people and your
kingdom. In Jesus's name. Amen.

If we love one another, God lives in us
and his love is made complete in us.
(1 John 4:12 NIV)

LIVE LIKE ANTHONY

- Make a list of your most important relationships. Start with your family, then your friends, then others (fellow church members, neighbors, coworkers, and so on).

- What are you consistently doing to invest in your most important relationships?

- Read 1 Corinthians 13. How can you daily demonstrate that kind of love in a practical way?

- How can you love others as Anthony did?

PHOTO
GALLERY

Anthony drinking coffee.

Anthony worshiping during a live recording.

Anthony leading worship at Restoration Church.

Anthony promoting Move the Mission with Dustin Williams at a Missouri district youth event.

Anthony with his wife, Lysandra, and their boys— Kingston, Davis, and Graham.

Anthony baptizing his oldest son, Kingston, with his father, Tom Trimble.

Anthony and Lysandra with their parents and their boys.
L to R: Diana Guerrero, Edward Guerrero, Lysandra Trimble, Davis Trimble, Kingston Trimble, Graham Trimble, Anthony Trimble, Debbie Trimble, and Tom Trimble.

Anthony with his dad in the office before church.

Anthony having fun with his dad.

Anthony with his mom, Debbie Trimble, and his siblings, Ryan Trimble and Stefani Nowack.

Anthony and his brother.

Anthony having coffee with his sister.

Anthony having coffee with his siblings.

Anthony and friends share a laugh with United Pentecostal Church International (UPCI) General Superintendent David K. Bernard.
L to R: Bradly DeLong, David K. Bernard, Dustin Williams, Anthony Trimble.

Anthony taking a more serious picture with UPCI General Superintendent David K. Bernard.
L to R: Bradly DeLong, David K. Bernard, Dustin Williams, Anthony Trimble.

Anthony with friends Jason Huckaby and Jason Staten during the
recording for the North American Youth Congress 2021
online worship service.

Anthony with friends Adam Shaw and Chris Green. Also pictured is
Adam's son, Judah.

Anthony and his dad sharing a meal with Chris Green.

Anthony and Lysandra with friends Matthew and Rebecca Johnson.

Anthony and Matthew Johnson.

Anthony and Lysandra with friends Bradly and Mariah DeLong.

Anthony and Bradly DeLong having coffee and working at Starbucks.

Anthony and Lysandra with friends Michael and Rebecca Ensey.

Anthony and Lysandra sharing a laugh with Michael and Rebecca Ensey.

Anthony with the Missouri district youth team and
former Missouri district youth presidents.
L to R: Steve Willeford, Matthew Johnson, Luke Levine, Dustin Williams,
Scott Graham, Aaron Batchelor, Chris Thornton, Anthony Trimble,
Nathan Santomieri, and Chuck Carr.

Anthony Trimble.

6

LISTEN

How to Focus on Others

———————◇———————

Matthew Johnson
LIFE LESSON:
Anthony taught us how to focus on others.

*Sometimes all a person wants is an
empathetic ear; all he or she needs is to talk it out.
Just offering a listening ear and an understanding heart
for his or her suffering can be a big comfort.*
—Roy T. Bennett

It was a warm, humid summer night on the Gulf Coast as our family pulled into the parking lot of Sunset Pointe Restaurant in Fairhope, Alabama. This local foodie favorite is located right on the water, and it is where all those searching via Yelp will see the five-star reviews. As we entered the restaurant we saw small lizards scurrying along the path, almost as if they were welcoming us back again to enjoy some fresh seafood. That night we had dinner on the patio with our special friends from out of town, Anthony and Lysandra Trimble, and their three wonderful boys.

Anthony and his family were passing through the area that weekend, and we were so excited to be taking them to one of our favorite restaurants. So much had happened since our last visit that we had a lot of catching up to do. Anthony had recently finished up a round of treatments and was feeling better. Nausea was no longer present and he felt alive and vibrant again. This trip was a hiatus from all the health concerns, and he used the opportunity to take his family out of town.

Winds of Pentecost, their church, was remodeling and setting up new equipment and protocols, and Anthony was right in the middle of it. Our conversation that night was a smorgasbord of topics: finding the right sound system for the sanctuary, setting up platform lighting, finding the best audio-visual-lighting consultants, and most of all, the myriad of challenges with leading a church.

During our time together I tried to ask Anthony about how things were going in his personal life and with his family, but each time he somehow managed to wiggle out of answering the question and instead asked how *our* family was doing.

Finally I said, "Anthony, I want to know how *you* are doing!"

His look said he knew he had been caught in his trickery and was going to have to talk about himself for a few minutes. This wasn't something new in my relationship with Anthony. This scenario happened each time we got together. He had a way of making a person feel as though he or she really mattered and that he truly cared. He always deflected attention away from himself and his own needs.

SELFLESSNESS

This trait Anthony carried with grace is called *selflessness*. It means caring about the needs of others more than one's own needs. While Anthony was battling cancer, expanding a church, growing a family, and serving as a district leader, he was still seeking ways in which he could bless others.

Selflessness is a rare trait in society today. Many care more about their own selves and their own kingdoms than they care about others. Thus, the opposite of being selfless is being selfish. Some call it narcissism. The main concern of these individuals is that their own wants and needs are satisfied. We all know people like this. They are known for their ego, their haughty look, their ability to talk endlessly about themselves, and their way of making others feel as though they don't matter. They view life as a competition: "How can I outdo the person I'm talking to?" These individuals have one mission: to ensure that others know who they are and what they have accomplished.

Anthony was the opposite of this. He didn't need his accomplishments flashing in lights. He didn't need the microphone or any attention for himself. He didn't need a particular position to feel valued in the kingdom of God. He simply wanted to use his talents for the Lord in any way possible.

SERVANT LEADERSHIP

Anthony's ministry was known all around the world. His music was played in churches, and videos of him leading worship were used as examples for how others should lead worship. Yet his singing was an accompaniment to his abilities as an anointed and powerful speaker.

For young leaders watching his life, I'm guessing many have wondered how he attained such influence. Perhaps it was from growing up in a pastor's home. Maybe he had gotten a "big break" in the music industry. Perhaps he had spent a lot of time with "guys at the top."

None of these were the case, however. He attained powerful influence through servant leadership—by putting others before himself. The Bible says, "Humble yourselves, therefore, under God's mighty hand, that he may lift you up in due time" (1 Peter 5:6 NIV). Much like the shepherd boy David, who had worked in the fields prior to being anointed as king, Anthony had put in his time serving in the "little ways."

SINCERELY LISTENING

My favorite example of this in the life of Anthony occurred during the time I was serving in Youth Ministries at the UPCI World Headquarters. Anthony would drive one of the vans during our annual mid-winter meetings in St. Louis. His job one week was very simple—to chauffeur district youth presidents and their spouses around St. Louis for meals or other group activities. When we asked him to help in this area, he was quick to comply without even asking for any specifics. He was excited about serving.

That particular year we had a major snowstorm, and driving a van around town was quite challenging. But Anthony never complained about a little snow and ice. He was actually laughing and having fun although the back of the van was swerving like a carnival ride. For youth presidents coming in from regions that never had snow or ice it was quite a ride—perhaps even a few moments of sheer terror! Thankfully, no one was injured that week, and everyone exited the vans with a smile. Anthony made sure of that.

During that week Anthony did his best *not* to get noticed. He was intentional about every moment he spent with this group. He was intentional with every conversation, listening intently and learning from the leaders he was serving. He wanted to get inside their minds and use that knowledge in his own ministry. Not once did he talk about himself or his accomplishments—he was always asking about others. Yet without trying he made a strong impression on many of those leaders, and in the years to come he would preach and sing at district youth conventions across the country.

CONCLUSION

We all want to make a difference in the world. We all want to accomplish things of importance. There isn't anything wrong with this. In fact, without goals a person cannot accomplish anything in this life. However, it is important that our desire to accomplish great things doesn't turn into a toxic formula for self-glorification or comparison with others. We all should remind ourselves of why we are here on this earth. The answer: to serve God and build his kingdom. It isn't about building our own kingdom.

This takes laying down personal pride and putting on humility. Scripture gives us direction on how to do this: Don't focus just on yourself: "Look not every man on his own things, but every man also on the things of others" (Philippians 2:4).

Put others above yourself: "Be kindly affectioned one to another with brotherly love; in honour preferring one another" (Romans 12:10). "Let nothing be done through strife or vainglory; but in lowliness of mind let each esteem other better than themselves" (Philippians 2:3).

Love others as you love yourself: "And the second is like, namely this, Thou shalt love thy neighbour as thyself. There is none other commandment greater than these" (Mark 12:31).

Pride is a destructive force, and unfortunately every person breathing will do battle with it. We can win only through the strength of God. I'm thankful for the life of Anthony Trimble because he exampled selflessness and humility to all of us. As you strive to live more like Anthony, think of the impact you can make on all those you meet.

LIVE LIKE ANTHONY

- Go into conversations looking to learn from your friends or colleagues.

- Start conversations by listening instead of talking.

- Stay curious, ask questions, and take good notes.

- When in a conversation, turn off electronic devices and truly listen.

- Treat all people with the same level of respect no matter their "status" or position.

———————◇———————

7

LEAD

How to Mentor a Friend

———◇———

Bradly DeLong
LIFE LESSON:
Anthony taught us how to mentor a friend.

*A mentor is someone who sees more
talent and ability within you
than you see in yourself and helps
bring it out of you.*
—Bob Proctor

I had never been to First Watch before, much less tried the Inspired Italian Omelet with a side of strawberries and their nine-grain wheat toast with jam. This was Anthony's spot, and this was his order. This was his place and his practice, and it quickly became mine as well. Truth be told, it was the location where the first of many of Anthony's habits and practices would be passed to me over the course of five years as he poured into my life more than he or I realized at the time. It also was the epicenter of where our friendship grew and the exact spot where my unofficial apprentice-ship began.

We started as friends and continued that way, but our relationship entered another dimension over time. We were fellow youth pastors, albeit a couple of years removed. We served in the same city, and we eventually ended up on the same team working together in the United Pente-costal Church International (UPCI) Missouri District Youth Department.

Our relationship took a turn shortly after Anthony's initial cancer diagnosis. It is remarkable to me that during a season in which his time grew more and more precious, he decided to spend it with me. Our friendship was sealed and immortalized across a table at First Watch with two Inspired Italian Omelets between us.

I recall arriving there early, anticipating our conversation. I was on a mission that day—to beat him to the restaurant, grab a table, sit with my friend, and encourage him as much as humanly possible as he faced the most formidable battle of his life. My goals were partially sunk that day when I discovered he was already there when I arrived. He had beaten me by a good twenty minutes. He did this nearly every time we met despite my best efforts to one-up him and arrive earlier.

Beyond that, I may have succeeded in being a help and an encouragement to him, but it seemed he was on the same exact mission, which was all the more remarkable considering his current battle. I remember thinking, *How is it that I'm leaving fuller than I came when my goal was to encourage him? How is he pouring into me more than I am pouring into him?*

Those questions were indicative of my time and relationship with Anthony Trimble. You see, whether by simple osmosis or by his focused, intentional approach, Anthony always seemed to pour more into my life than I could ever reciprocate. That has never been more apparent than now as I reflect on all that I learned from him. Many times he did it in a subtle manner and by leading through example. Other times he did it by leading with focused intention and a targeted goal.

The notion that certain personalities and characteristics are contagious is compelling, and Anthony's seemed to be the most contagious of all. Seemingly without fail, his spirit of excellence and his lifestyle of service and devotion would bleed into the lives of those around him, including my own. His was one of the most transmissible and infectious personalities I have ever met, and I'm thankful to have been in close-enough proximity to glean from him. He was very much a friend to me, but he also was very much a mentor.

I have heard it said that your relationship with an individual is largely based on how you feel about yourself when you are around the person and after you leave his or her presence. If this premise is the case, it is no wonder that Anthony had such a following of people who desired to spend time with him. On a personal level, I always seemed to feel better about myself by the time I left the table with him, hung up the phone after talking to him, or wrapped up a long event for Missouri Youth—really, just working alongside him. It seemed that no matter the setting or the context, he always managed to pour into my life, to teach, to encourage, or simply to inspire me to want to be better.

To this day I recognize the significant imprint he had on my life, even in the little things. Examples include sending voice memos through iMessage to save time and to communicate more quickly. My family and peers have Anthony to thank for that!

He taught me that Albanese Gummy Bears were unmatched in the realm of gummies and that it is acceptable to pair them with a can of Coca-Cola despite the high sugar content and subsequent sugar crash. He demonstrated for me that a fedora hat can be stylish, although I was never brave enough to try to pull one off as he could.

He drilled into me the spirit of excellence when it came to district youth events, ministries, and functions as well as events at the local church level. He taught me never to settle for anything subpar or to give a halfhearted effort, a lesson we will discuss later. Additionally, as he lived within boundaries, exemplifying to me the importance of family—one of the most important lessons I learned from him was the prioritization of my spouse and children, plus the ministry boundaries that ought to reinforce those priorities.

Whether directly or indirectly, he was always teaching me, and, among the other lessons I have already listed, these are the lessons I learned from my friend who became my mentor.

HIS INVESTMENT OF TIME

Anthony invested his time into others. Upon contemplating it further, I recognize that the most precious thing Anthony had to give in life was his time. The sobering truth was that he had less time to give than most, but he chose to invest it into others, including me.

One of the first times we met was in between his cancer treatments. His time was more valuable than ever before. He had limited time to recoup from treatment, spend time with family, serve at the church, record albums and music, work on district youth events, maintain the day-to-day business of life, and work on the many projects with which he was engaged. You get the picture. Time was as precious a commodity to Anthony as it could be, but he strategically invested that time into friends and followers like me.

I mentioned earlier that Anthony was always on time, often twenty minutes early, and he would use that time while waiting on me to invest in others, whether over the phone or in the restaurant itself. But while I was there he was wholeheartedly engaged. He was not on his phone or otherwise distracted; he was focused and intentional (there's that word again), and we would often spend a couple hours together discussing everything from family to ministry, music, and St. Louis Cardinals baseball.

Beyond our breakfast meetings he would spend one-on-one time with me at Missouri District events. We would call one another regularly and talk for extended periods of time. We even took a couple of road trips together, during which Anthony maximized his driving time by investing in his friends, sharing spiritual truths, laughing over humorous stories, and unwittingly imparting his contagious spirit and nature.

It certainly goes without saying that the most precious gift he gave me and others was the investment of the thing he seemed to value the most: *time*. Because he valued his time so much, he was extremely careful about how he utilized it, how he stewarded it, and where he spent it. The way he valued his time emphasizes just how much of an investment it was and continues to be, one that I'm hoping will see an eternal and ample return.

What he truly demonstrated and what I have come to realize is that investing your time in people, in friends, in family, and in someone who is not as far down the road as you are is one of the most worthwhile investments you can give. A prime example of that truth is my friendship with Anthony and everything I gleaned from him along the way. The time he invested in me continues paying dividends in my life, and I'm certain that many others could say the same. I thank God that Anthony invested his time.

HIS SPIRIT OF EXCELLENCE

Anthony also shared and invested his spirit of excellence. If you knew Anthony, you know he settled for nothing less than excellence, whether it was at the local church level, district youth ministry, or otherwise. If the final product, the event, the design, or the service was not excellent or proved to be lacking in any way, Anthony did not shy away from correcting it.

In fact, on more than one occasion at an event or district gathering I would hear him say, "That's not Missouri Youth. That's not what we do. "What he meant by that was the simple fact that we had a standard, a benchmark to reach— one that would honor God and serve others—and we were not going to settle for anything subpar. This attitude of excellence was part of the spirit Anthony exhibited, and that spirit drove me and others to want to be better.

Anthony wanted the absolute best for the kingdom and subsequently for the people around him. He demonstrated that desire by giving his absolute best, even when he hardly had the strength to do anything at all. Whether he was preaching, singing, writing, serving, or pouring into his friend over breakfast, he did it with all his might and with all the tenacity he could muster. Anthony always seemed to give his best to others, including me.

On one occasion he told me that due to the sickness in his body he didn't feel as if he had enough strength to preach at a church that had invited him to come. Still, he told me that he felt the Lord had called him to minister to them. When he arrived, he was still very weak but was determined to preach and give his all, no matter how little his strength was at the moment. He recalled later that the Lord miraculously strengthened him, and he was able to minister as though he had no weakness at all.

Even cancer could not stop Anthony from exemplifying excellence, and his sickness never became an "out" or an excuse for him to give a halfhearted effort or to invest less of himself into others than he felt necessary. Truthfully, if the rest of us "put our best foot forward," Anthony seemed to have two "best" feet. In other words, he never seemed to settle for the lesser option or the lesser "foot." He was wholeheartedly excellent, and his pursuit of excellence was passed intentionally—even unintentionally—to those around him, including me.

HIS SACRIFICIAL INVESTMENT

Anthony always gave his best and invested himself sacrificially into others. The truth is that mentoring someone else always involves pouring yourself into that individual as well as pouring what you have learned from God, from his Word, and from life experiences into that open vessel. The further truth is that discipling, mentoring, and bringing someone else alongside can entail a great sacrifice on your behalf, one that you must willingly choose to offer.

With that said, it has occurred to me that Anthony could have spent his time, as precious and valuable as it was, investing in any number of other areas. What is most sobering is that he took the time to invest it, along with himself, in me. Peers often invest equally into one another. If that is the case, Anthony was more a mentor than a peer, because I see no scenario in which my investment into him equaled his investment into me.

At face value, that seems like a net loss for him. When you pour out more than you receive, you cannot quantify or reconcile the return. However, the values of the kingdom supersede all others, which is why investing into someone who cannot immediately reciprocate is entirely appropriate. That is exactly what Jesus did during his earthly ministry and what he continues doing today.

Anthony invested himself sacrificially into others, and in doing so he typified Christ, just as he did in so many other ways. It is no wonder that both our mantra and our mission have been to "live like Anthony." Anthony lived like Jesus. Without reservation or self-preservation, he poured himself into others, and we are ongoing beneficiaries of his investment.

His sacrificial investment was never more apparent to me than when I received a voice memo from him that was one of the last messages we shared over the phone. He was weak, and cancer had taken a toll on his body. Still, he had enough strength to pick up his phone, record a message, and tell his friend that he loved him and was praying for him. I have recently thought that if that moment doesn't remind me of Jesus's heart for others in his own last hours, I do not know what does.

Even as Jesus breathed some of his final breaths, he looked to the benefit and care of others. He pardoned the thief. He prayed for those gambling for his garments. He provided for his mother and entrusted her into the care of his beloved disciple. He invested into those around him without regard for himself. (See Luke 23:33–43; John 19:25–27.)

With that picture and example in mind, one cannot help but see the parallel and the same spirit in the life of Anthony Trimble. Even at his lowest he found a way to invest himself into others, especially those within his own family. Beyond that, he even found a way to invest in friends and followers like me. In fact, just hours before his passing he got a message to me through a family member—one that I will never forget. It was a simple acknowledgment of his love for a friend, one that stirs me to this day even as I write about his exceptional life and leadership.

CONCLUSION

Anthony was my friend. He was a friend who lived like Jesus, a friend who invested his time, his spirit, and himself into others, and a friend who poured more into me than I could ever hope to repay. He was a friend who gave selflessly and inspired me to be better. He provided a friendship that I hope to emulate for someone else. Anthony was a friend who became a mentor.

LIVE LIKE ANTHONY

- Write the names of three friends whom you can actively invest in as a mentor.

- Write down several ways through which you can actively invest in those individuals. How can you invest your time, wisdom, resources, and experiences?

- Schedule time to meet with each of the three you listed. Invite them out for coffee or for lunch. Take them to First Watch if you have one close by.

PART THREE

Kingdom Impact

---◇---

The kingdom of God is a spiritual kingdom that is manifested only where there is submission to the authority of the King. This kingdom was inaugurated in Jesus Christ and currently is manifested through the church. The movement of the kingdom is revealed as the unfolding of God's redemptive plan for humanity through the power of the gospel. Anthony gave himself wholly to the expansion of the kingdom of God. It was his life.

*For the Kingdom of God is not a matter
of what we eat or drink, but of living a life of goodness
and peace and joy in the Holy Spirit.*
(Romans 14:17 NLT)

*The Kingdom of Heaven is like a treasure that
a man discovered hidden in a field. In his
excitement, he hid it again and sold everything he
owned to get enough money to buy the field.*
(Matthew 13:44 NLT)

---◇---

8

WORDSMITH

The Power of the Pen

Jason Huckaby
LIFE LESSON:
Anthony taught us the power of the pen.

*If you want to be an authentic writer,
learn to tell the truth, to wrestle with it,
to reflect on it, and then to write about
it with great care and great humility.*
—Vinita Hampton Wright

I cannot think of summer seasons in Tennessee without remembering weeks spent at Camp Lake Benson. They are a thing of legend. Great services. Great preaching. Pranks. Rocking chairs on the landing. Softball and basketball. Memories of meeting people and making friends. These are just a few of the things every former camper and worker recalls every time the month of June rolls around. Tennessee Youth Camp built ministries and memories that are hard to forget even as time moves on.

Everyone has a story. I have many, but there's one I'm thankful for even to this day. My introduction to Anthony was the result of the youth camp talent show. This too was a yearly Friday night tradition. Anticipation built all week as students signed up to showcase their talents—or signed up their friends unaware. They played out as most talent shows do.

After the performance a panel of "judges" discussed what we all had just seen and heard. I was instructed to respond to each of the acts with a degree of satire, to which I humbly obliged. Anthony was part of a band made up of campers called "God About." They performed at the show, and my comments followed. I cannot recall what I said in the moment, but whatever it was struck a creative chord in Anthony. In response to my satirical evaluation, he wrote a song that would echo through Camp Lake Benson for years to come.

The camp ballad said, "Huck-A-Bay, you are so Ug-A-Lay!" I could not enter a room without hearing a camper yell that back to me. That summer I quickly learned the power of Anthony's pen and his words. His words prayed powerful prayers. His pen wrote songs and sermons. Through his pen he brought to life preaching, praise anthems, plans, and vision.

SPIRITUAL INSPIRATION

Anthony was a dynamic wordsmith unrivaled in his ability to connect Word and Spirit. He knew that the Spirit gives divine inspiration and power to the pen. Songs and sermons can be written, but they must be infused with the Spirit in order to be effectual. Because of his Spirit-led life, the songs he penned and the sermons he wrote powerfully demonstrated the God with whom he walked. Perhaps like the psalmist David on the back side of a desert, fighting the elements for a lamb, Anthony taught us there is nothing we cannot overcome if we have a fight and a song.

The Spirit guided him when he prayed, guiding his pen as he drafted sermons. The Spirit led him as he wrote powerful lyrics. Anthony knew it was not him praying—it was the Spirit making intercession. He knew it was not merely his words as he built sermons—God was providing the words and the direction. He knew it was not simply him rhyming words and compiling songs—it was through the inspiration of the Spirit.

His experiences and the Spirit guided his efforts. Anthony knew and often talked about how the Spirit became the divine inspiration for the words he wrote, preached, and prayed. He knew how to pray. He could write a song. He could put a sermon together. That seems like an understatement to anyone who knew him. But he knew it was the Spirit generating the power. This is what made him a dynamic, unrivaled worship leader. It was not just the words he sang; he was connected to a supernatural pen.

When he began praying, singing lyrics, or preaching a sermon, the Spirit gave value to the words. In the process, the Spirit brought supernatural strength to the worshiper and the listener because the Spirit always moved. Anthony knew that all that mattered was that the Spirit moved and worked through him. He was a vessel willing to be used by God. The intimate union of his abilities and the Spirit brought power to his pen.

This is what happened when Anthony prayed. This is what happened when Anthony wrote songs. This is what happened when Anthony prepared sermons. This is what he let happen and what he wanted to happen. If it is true that the Spirit gives inspiration, how did this play out in Anthony's life? How do these truths apply to Anthony? I'm glad you asked.

PRAYERS

Anthony was a person of prayer, and his prayers connected him to the Spirit. At the beginning of this journey he called me. The call came after the doctors had delivered the diagnosis in which they gave him three to five years to live. He said, "Huck, the doctor explained that my diagnosis could be compared to averages in a classroom. Think of it like this. You have a classroom full of fifth-graders. If the average grade on an assignment is 80 percent, that means half of the class made a 60, and half the class made a 100. That is how you determine the average."

The doctor told Anthony the average lifespan with a diagnosis of stage-four cancer was three to five years and explained that if Anthony was a "60," he had three years left. If he was a "100," he had five. I remember telling him in that moment, "Anthony, you are way above average." Anthony prayed. I prayed. People all over the world began taking him before the Lord in prayer. Those prayers connected to the Spirit. He called me the day he passed the five-year mark and said, "I've officially outlived my diagnosis!" He lived almost six years after his diagnosis. Anthony is still an example that the words you pray are more powerful than a doctor's diagnosis.

As time went on and the journey continued, we prayed before every surgery. We prayed before every visit to the doctor. We prayed after every victory. We prayed after every update. Anthony knew and showed us by example that the words we pray have power. This remained true toward the end as my family and I visited him at their house a few days before he passed away.

As I knelt beside him, Anthony opened up about feeling his transition from this life to the next. He told me, "God has answered so many of my prayers through this process. There has been one miracle after the other." His tumor had been in a strategic place that made surgery a possibility. In addition, his drug therapy had caused enough of the cancer to disappear so they could go through with the surgery.

Throughout it all Anthony prayed. His words, coupled with the Spirit, had power. From diagnosis to surgeries to the strength that he felt to lead worship and preach camps, the Spirit strengthened him every step of the way. The Lord answered the prayers he prayed. There is power in the words you pray in your prayer room.

SONGS

Prayer was just one of the places Anthony's words had power. He also serves as an example of someone led by the Spirit in the songs he wrote. Anthony, as well as his dad (Pastor Tom Trimble), always had a way of leading people into the presence of the Lord. They knew that music and worship were about more than simply singing a song.

During one of our last conversations I said to Anthony, "I was listening to your music on the drive to your house, and your new project has the song 'He Can.' It reminds me a lot of your dad." Anthony had the same gifting and ability as his father. He could take his generation into the presence of the Lord.

We saw Anthony's faith and connection to the Spirit in that song and the many others he sang. They were not merely lyrics about his walk with God; they were Spirit-inspired and experience-driven words that took the listener on a journey into the presence of God for hope, healing, restoration, and strength.

David's songs drove away the evil spirit inflicting emotional and spiritual pain on Saul. The words in the shepherd's songs were so rich in the Holy Spirit that they had authority over demonic spirits. The shepherd's experience brought the power. Like David, Anthony also had experiences. He understood that when he walked into a sanctuary to lead worship, he drove away spirits that would cause anxiety, fear, and depression. The power of pen and lyrics created a fertile field where the seed of the Word could be planted.

The objective was to usher the listener into the presence of the Lord. The Spirit helped him record multiple albums while fighting sickness. The power of Anthony's lyrical pen was a healing agent to every worshiper and an inspiration to every prayer closet. There was power in his pen.

SERMONS

Anthony was a person of prayer and one of the great worship leaders and songwriters of our time. He was no novice in the pulpit either. He preached in camps and conventions across America. On more than one occasion he called me to discuss notes and ideas as he prepared to stand and inspire a generation of people to cultivate spiritual disciplines and good works.

We once had a conversation about the pressure to find something clever and engaging in order to pique the interest of a youthful congregation. I recalled a time when I was praying about preaching at youth camps in the summer and I asked the Lord to give me a word for our generation. I did not want to just go through the motions of preaching another sermon. In that moment of prayer the Lord spoke three words to me: "I still speak!" God still speaks. We can have divine inspiration in our lyrics, sermons, and the prayers we pray because God still speaks. Anthony and I settled on one principle: it is not the clever, inspiring story that changes lives; it is the coalescence of the Spirit and the word that produces the necessary climate to initiate change.

Anthony was preaching out somewhere, as he often did even in the midst of his battle, when he told me that while he was preaching, the service just kind of exploded and the Holy Ghost moved in. In his own selfless way he told me that he didn't know if he necessarily preached well (we know he did!), but what he did know was that there was a move of God, and many people received the gift of the Holy Ghost.

Anthony knew it was not about his own abilities. What mattered was that God had shown up. It was a supernatural moment. It did not happen because of his strength. Part of what Anthony learned through his sickness was that he had to rely on something that was beyond himself. For him to walk to the pulpit and preach took a touch of the Spirit on him physically. The power in his sermons came from the Spirit.

As a young man I played golf on my school team. My golf coach tried to teach me how to drive the ball, but with every swing it seemed the ball traveled only a short distance. Across the way a golf veteran, probably in his late seventies, consistently hit the ball a lot farther than I did. My coach asked, "Do you see that elderly man hitting the ball? Do you think he's stronger than you?" I was 6'4" tall and weighed in at 285 pounds, so the answer was no. The coach went on to say the difference is not in the strength but in letting the club do the work.

I learned a lesson on that golf course that has stuck with me in ministry to this day. Our failure, often in the pulpit but in other areas as well, is that we are trying to achieve things by our own strength. On the golf course the club is supposed to do the work. In preaching the Word of God is supposed to do the work. His Word spoke the world into existence, healed blind eyes, unstopped deaf ears, raised the dead, and inspired the first-century church. It is incumbent upon us to understand that the Word still works. Anthony understood this, and that understanding allowed him to be a great preacher. There was power in his pen.

CONCLUSION

Anthony taught us that the power in his pen was from the Spirit moving through him. His prayers, lyrics, and sermons were Spirit-led. He was sick, and there were times when his strength was so small that he could not physically pray, sing, or preach on his own. But he was effective because the Spirit was working through him. There was power in the pen.

The apostle Paul declared,

For what the law could not do, in that it was weak through the flesh, God sending his own Son in the likeness of sinful flesh, and for sin, condemned sin in the flesh: That the righteousness of the law might be fulfilled in us, who walk not after the flesh, but after the Spirit. For they that are after the flesh do mind the things of the flesh; but they that are after the Spirit the things of the Spirit.
(Romans 8:3–5)

Anthony taught us through his prayers. He taught us through his songs. He taught us through his sermons. He followed after the Spirit. He was a living example. In the same chapter of Romans Paul wrote,

Likewise the Spirit also helps in our weaknesses. For we do not know what we should pray for as we ought, but the Spirit Himself makes intercession for us with groanings which cannot be uttered. Now He who searches the hearts knows what the mind of the Spirit is, because He makes intercession for the saints according to the will of God.
(Romans 8:26–27 NKJV)

Another translation states it this way:

In the same way, the Spirit helps us in our weakness.
We do not know what we ought to pray for, but the
Spirit himself intercedes for us through wordless groans.
And he who searches our hearts knows the mind of the
Spirit, because the Spirit intercedes for God's people in
accordance with the will of God.
(Romans 8:26–27 NIV)

Anthony learned through the weakness of his flesh that we must follow after the leading of the Spirit because the Spirit provides the power. Anthony showed me the power of his pen that June evening in Dickson, Tennessee, at a youth camp. We became and stayed great friends, and he continued showing me as he lived, fought, and ultimately won the race.

The flesh was weak, but the Spirit was strong in him. He produced his greatest prayers, his greatest songs, and his greatest sermons in crisis. Despite the fact that his flesh was weak, there was still power in the pen because of the Spirit. His life provided a blueprint for all of us to follow. I can still hear it clearly: "Huck-A-Bay!" There is power in the pen.

LIVE LIKE ANTHONY

- There also is power in *your* pen. I challenge you to let the Spirit of God and the Word of God inspire you to write.

- Purchase a journal and make a daily commitment to write down the things the Lord leads you to write.

- Write out your prayers and also record your testimonies of victory, healing, and deliverance.

- Write a worship song in honor of Anthony. Who knows? It may be the next big chart-topper.

- Write out a sermon that is inspired by the life of Anthony.

9

WORSHIPER

The Power of Worship

———◇———

Michael Ensey
LIFE LESSON:
Anthony taught us the power of worship.

*We must never rest until everything
within us worships God.*
—A. W. Tozer

All of life is worship. Every thought, word, and action represents a spiritual transaction in which we offer the sacrifice of our time, energy, and focus. For Anthony Trimble, worship was more than a church responsibility or a scheduled activity. It was his daily lifestyle. Any description of him that did not include "worshiper" would be wholly inadequate and incomplete. Yes, he was a legendary songwriter and worship leader, but worship was not just something he did. It was who he was. Anthony was a worshiper.

SETTING THE STAGE

Two of my favorite memories of Anthony involved two of the biggest stages upon which he worshiped as he led others into the presence of God. In the spring of 2015 I asked Anthony to lead the worship team at the UPCI Youth Ministry Training Event, which was scheduled to take place in August 2016 in Nashville. In November 2015 he received his initial diagnosis of cancer. Months later we discussed whether or not he should honor his commitment. He was undergoing treatment. He was weak and unsure if he would be able to be at his best. Several months before the event he made up his mind—he would do it with the help of the Lord.

He led a dynamic worship team that weekend. He even wrote an original song to kick off the event and introduce the theme of the conference: "Create." The title of his song was "All I Am."

I was created, I was created to love You, To love You
I was created, I was created to love You, To love You
As I sing will You open up the heavens
My delight is just being in Your presence

I will bless the Lord at all times
I will bless the Lord at all times
Every breath, All I am is Yours

I was created, I was created to praise You, To praise You
I was created, I was created to praise You
As we sing will You open up the heavens
My delight is just being in Your presence

I will bless the Lord at all times
I will bless the Lord at all times
Every breath, All I am
I will praise Your name forever
I will praise Your name forever
Every breath, All I am is Yours

Shout it out
This is why I was made
To bring glory to Your name
This is why I was made
To bring glory to Your name[17]

The message of this song was Anthony's life. He was created to worship his Creator. We had an incredible time of prayer for Anthony at the conclusion of that event. The worship team, special guest speakers, event leaders, and conference attendees gathered around him on the stage. It was pure. It was powerful. We all knew God had touched him; there was no doubt in our minds that God was doing a work of healing in his body.

God did touch him. After Anthony's original diagnosis, his doctor was reluctant to perform surgery because there were so many cancerous lesions on his liver that he felt surgery would be unproductive. The outlook was not very positive or hopeful, but the church was praying. After months of chemotherapy, his doctor informed him that the chemo couldn't do any more for him. He was no longer making any progress, and cancer was ravaging his body. Anthony

---

17. "All I Am" (Weldon Music Publishing, 2016).

decided to stop the treatment and instead focus on natural remedies and prayer—always prayer.

Months later they did another scan and discovered the lesions were significantly reduced, so his doctor finally agreed to allow the surgery. Hope was being restored. In May 2017 Anthony was about to undergo this major surgery during which they would remove part of his liver and part of his colon. Before the surgery they did a colonoscopy to create a reference point to pinpoint exactly where the tumor was so it could easily be identified during surgery. But the colonoscope did not find the tumor in his colon! All they saw was what they described as a "tattoo" of where the tumor had been. (They had marked the approximate location of the tumor during a previous procedure.) It was a miracle of healing!

Two months later Anthony was singing on another major stage. He was part of the worship team at North American Youth Congress in July 2017. For the first time that event was being held in a football stadium—Lucas Oil Stadium in Indianapolis. The opening night I preached about the "Faith Factor." I declared that fear may be present, but it doesn't have to be a factor when we have faith in God. Anthony lived out that truth every day of his life, especially during his sickness. He shared his testimony of healing during the last night of the event. Over 34,000 young people thundered in worship, heaven applauded, and hell quaked in fear as we celebrated this great victory. He shared his testimony as he sang about a faithful God who keeps his promises. He is a God who can move mountains and make a way when there is no way. You can find his testimony on YouTube. Search: "Anthony Trimble NAYC Testimony."

A LIVING SACRIFICE

The setting of those two stages provided an incredible platform for Anthony to worship God, but I believe they pale in comparison to Anthony's greatest stage—the platform of his daily life. He lived out the challenge of the apostle Paul to the church in Rome. Anthony was a living sacrifice.

I appeal to you therefore, brothers,
by the mercies of God, to present your bodies as a living
sacrifice, holy and acceptable to God, which is your spiritual
worship. Do not be conformed to this world,
but be transformed by the renewal of your mind, that by
testing you may discern what is the will of God, what is
good and acceptable and perfect.
(Romans 12:1–2 ESV)

Long before David was ever a king, he was a worshiper. He was the sweet psalmist of Israel and the Bible's worship leader. His songs—the psalms—have so much meaning because they were not the product of a songwriting session in Jerusalem's recording studio. He wrote these songs while walking through the valley of the shadow of death. He wrote them while fleeing for his life and hiding in caves. He wrote them in the wilderness and on the battlefield. His songs mean so much to us because he was living the words that he penned.

I will bless the Lord at all times: his praise
shall continually be in my mouth. . . . I sought the Lord,
and he heard me, and delivered me from all my fears. . . .
This poor man cried, and the Lord heard him,
and saved him out of all his troubles.
(Psalm 34:1, 4, 6)

So it was with Anthony, the sweet psalmist of St. Charles. His sermons and his songs mean so much to us because he was living the words of those songs! He was a true worshiper; he worshiped in spirit and in truth. When there were no answers, there was worship. When there were no more words, there was worship. When he didn't even know what to pray, there was worship. Anthony declared—

I will live to bring You praise
Lord You give and take away
I will glorify Your name
Every hour come what may
Come what may
Come what may[18]

These words mean something to us because they were not carefully crafted in the confines of comfort but were forged in the fire of adversity. Anthony's motivation was never popularity or promotion. He never sought a big stage. His only motivation for writing, singing, ministering, and preaching was bringing glory to God and seeing transformation in the lives of others.

---

18. "Come What May" (Weldon Music Publishing, 2020).

PERFECTED PRAISE

Jesus provided his own personal commentary of Psalm 8 by introducing the concept of perfected praise: "Yea; have ye never read, Out of the mouth of babes and sucklings thou hast perfected praise?" (Matthew 21:16). Perfected praise does not come from a source of strength or a position of power. The source of perfected praise is that helpless one who is completely dependent on another for every life-giving necessity. There is something about our dependent weaknesses that gives opportunity for the strength of God to be perfected and for his glory to be revealed.

Jesus was referencing a psalm of King David: "Out of the mouth of babes and sucklings hast thou ordained strength because of thine enemies, that thou mightest still the enemy and the avenger" (Psalm 8:2). God perfects praise by ordaining strength from that which is completely dependent upon him. There is victory over our enemies in that kind of worship! We find echoes of this concept in Paul's writings:

But he said to me, "My grace is sufficient for you, for my power is made perfect in weakness." Therefore I will boast all the more gladly of my weaknesses, so that the power of Christ may rest upon me.
(2 Corinthians 12:9 ESV)

Anthony's strength was found not in his natural abilities but rather in his dependence upon God. His anointing was the result of his reliance upon God. This word *perfected* used by Jesus in Matthew 21 means "to complete thoroughly;

to repair; to restore." Perfected praise, or dependent praise, produces restoration. One of Anthony's final acts of worship was to work with his father, Pastor Tom Trimble, to rename and rebrand his home church from Winds of Pentecost to Restoration Church. Restoration Church now stands as a memorial to Anthony's perfected praise. It is a place of worship where many lives are restored in the presence of God through the power of the gospel.

THE ELEMENTS OF WORSHIP

In Genesis 22 God tempted Abraham and called him to offer his promised son, Isaac, as a sacrifice on Mount Moriah. As they neared the mountain of sacrifice, Abraham gave his servants this description of their intended purpose: "Stay here with the donkey; I and the boy will go over there and worship and come again to you" (Genesis 22:5 ESV). Abraham recognized that what he was doing was indeed worship unto God. He demonstrated his faith in God by obeying this command that made no sense to his carnal way of reasoning. The first element of worship we see in this passage is obedient faith.

By faith Abraham, when he was tested,
offered up Isaac, and he who had received the promises
was in the act of offering up his only son, of whom it was
said, "Through Isaac shall your offspring be named."
He considered that God was able even to raise him from
the dead, from which, figuratively speaking,
he did receive him back.
(Hebrews 11:17–19 ESV)

It is believed that Isaac was a full-grown young man at the time when God tempted Abraham.[19] The context certainly supports this view. Isaac was old enough to understand the proper sacrificial process and recognize that they had fire and wood but no animal to sacrifice. He also was old enough to go on a three-to-four-day journey with his aged father and strong enough to carry all the wood for the burnt sacrifice. If all of this is true, then I think it would be reasonable to assume that Isaac was strong enough to resist being sacrificed if he had wanted to. I believe it was an act of submission on Isaac's part to allow his father to bind him and place him upon that altar. The second element of worship is complete submission.

Together Abraham and Isaac demonstrated the final element of worship—total trust. They trusted God and they trusted each other. Their trust ultimately produced a miraculous outcome. God had already provided a ram that was caught in the thicket. God knew that he could trust both Abraham and Isaac with the covenant promise.

CONCLUSION

Anthony lived out these elements of worship: obedient faith, complete submission, and total trust. He expressed this spiritual act of worship in every area of his life, especially in his relationships and through his ministry. He was completely committed to his God-given calling and fully submitted to the plan of God even when there were more questions than answers. In the final days of his life he lifted his hands in worship until he didn't have the strength to do it anymore.

19. Josephus, "Concerning Isaac the Legitimate Son of Abraham," *Antiquities of the Jews,* ccel.org/ccel/josephus/complete/complete.ii.ii.xiii.html

Then he lifted his voice in worship until he didn't have the strength to do that anymore either. Finally he hummed in worship when that was all he could do. He trusted God and he worshiped until his final breath. Anthony was a worshiper.

LIVE LIKE ANTHONY

- What does a "lifestyle of worship" mean to you and how can you live out this concept?

- What does a "living sacrifice" mean to you and how can you be an example of this concept in your daily life?

- What is a creative way that you can worship God today?

- How has Anthony Trimble's life inspired you to be a worshiper?

10

WORLD-CHANGER

The Power of Music

———◇———

Jeremy Painter
LIFE LESSON:
Anthony taught us the power of music.

Music will help dissolve your perplexities and purify
your character and sensibilities, and in time of care and
sorrow, will keep a fountain of joy alive in you.
—Dietrich Bonhoeffer

What is music? For most of my life I never thought to ask. When I was a child, music was to me just one of the great *things* in life, like food, water, mountains, and stars. Music could alter the atmosphere of a room. It could make melancholy men dance and happy men cry. Old men told me that when they heard a certain song from their youth it was like being in a time machine that made them feel young and old at the same time.

Music pervaded most of what we did. When Mom put us to sleep, she would sing a lullaby or turn on soft piano music. When we turned on the radio in the morning, there was music; when we played games at school, there was music; when we went to a restaurant, there was music. When we weren't thinking about much at all, we hummed. When Dad came home from work, he played the piano. At church we sang before we preached, and we sang again when the preaching was done. Every important event was solemnized by music. Funerals and weddings, memorials and holidays, birthdays and baptisms—music, music, music. If an alien from Mars had been observing us, he might have thought we had more in common with birds than any other species on Earth.

I still don't have a definitive answer to the question "What is music?" It helps me to think of it sometimes as liquid architecture (or of architecture as frozen music). Music occupies a liminal space—not quite pure spirit, not quite pure matter but somewhere on the border between the two. Perhaps it is one of the original powers of creation, close somehow to the heart of God. The ancient Greeks associated music with divinity. The very word *music* stems from *Muse*, the Greek name for nine goddesses. The ancient Hebrew poet who wrote the book of Job said that the "morning stars" sang with the angels while Elohim laid the foundations of the earth. (See Job 38:4–7.)

But there's one other characteristic of music I would like to mention—the characteristic I've observed especially in relation to Anthony.

On the day Laura and I were married, a friend brought a video recorder—a rare luxury in the mid-nineties—to record the ceremony and the reception. The first time I watched the video, I was delighted that he had taken the time to do this, but I thought it was a bit eccentric of him, for instance, to pan away from the wedding party and the guests to intermittently track the flight of birds flying low across the nearby Puget Sound. As I viewed the film I was left with the impression that my friend was a bit bored at times with the wedding. A few months later, though, he gave me another version of the film. "This one," he said, "I've added music to."

When I watched this version it was as if I were watching a completely different wedding. With the swelling music in the background, I was no longer watching just an event; I was watching an epic pageant worthy of the great poets and prophets. Angels, not men and women, glided down the aisle and took their places at my side. As the score rose to a crescendo, a being clothed in white light appeared. Beauty itself stepped down the aisle with her father. Her train, attended by cherubs and seraphs, filled the temple. At the end of the ceremony, glowing images of God recessed arm in arm through a portal (previously known to me as the church's back door), striding toward the marriage supper of the bride and groom. And there they sang and laughed and talked, coats flung over their shoulders, looking out upon the sea. And the flight of the birds that had seemed a distraction in my first viewing now evoked scenes from Genesis 1, as if I were now watching the fifth and sixth days of creation. I hadn't remembered our wedding that way. It was hard to believe I had even been there, much less that I had been the groom.

I entertained for a moment the idea that the music in the background had *elevated* our wedding, but I quickly dismissed the idea. That was a wholly inadequate explanation for what I had just witnessed. The music was not the *cause* of the glory I had seen; the music merely *revealed* the glory that had already been present on that day. Music had cleared the fog that hid the glory of our lives; it pulled back the veil to reveal the truth, the essence, the soul of that great day. Music revealed the divinity of the moment. It took me to the top of a kind of mount of transfiguration where I beheld, as it were, Moses and Elijah conversing with our wedding party.

This is music's nature. Truths reach their ultimate expression in this world when they're expressed in music. This is why hymns are so powerful, and this is why poetry (which captures the musical quality of words themselves) is able to say so much while saying so little. There are just some things that only music can say.

This brings me to Anthony.

I didn't get to spend much time with him. I lived in the Pacific Northwest and caught a glimpse of him only when he was a fourteen-year-old boy playing the drums for his parents at a district youth convention. I moved to St. Charles, Missouri, in 2019. But at that point Anthony was in his mid-thirties, just as cancer was beginning to make it very difficult for him to socialize. Other than getting to spend one afternoon with him at a Shakespeare play (and sharing the same birthday, September 10), life didn't afford us the luxury of our becoming close friends. But I did observe him carefully over the last two years of his life.

What struck me during that time (and strikes me still) was that he had lived the kind of life in his youth that promised the greatest of lives in middle age and beyond. He was beloved by all who knew him. He had earned everyone's respect. He was no man's enemy (no easy feat, I'm told, for a church music director). He had managed to be true to his apostolic heritage and yet be universally admired. He was already wise as a young man. And it seemed to me that he had made the kinds of decisions on a day-to-day basis throughout his youth that gave him the very rare capacity for a life of genuine happiness and holiness.

But like everyone else, I struggled to come to grips with the notion that at not quite thirty-six years of age, Anthony's life was complete. His excellent youth seemed like a pediment upon which to erect a masterpiece of marble. There was so much good to come, it seemed to me. But no sooner had that pediment been meticulously constructed and brought to its finest polish and prepared to uphold the statue of a legend, cancer came. Without explanation, the sculpture was decommissioned. Rays of sunlight streamed into a massive hall through lofty windows overhead, illuminating an enigma: a grand pediment sitting silent and alone with no sculpture atop it.

Old age tends to humble us and remove from us the illusion of independence. And it is on these terms that old age tends to expertly prepare us to meet God. The truth is, though, that by his mid-thirties Anthony already possessed these qualities. If life in this world and in our mortal bodies is meant to prepare us to meet our God, Anthony's life was anything but unfinished. We didn't get to see the traits Anthony cultivated in his youth flower into a resplendent old age, but we did get to see what it would have been like to witness the faith of one of God's champions. His life was a song—a song that revealed the glory of faith, the refusal to give voice to despair.

There are three moments that cross my mind when I think of him—moments that are now as much a part of my mental picture of him as the name "Anthony."

PERFECTION IN WEAKNESS

The first moment occurred after I had finished teaching one Wednesday night. The subject of the lesson was the blessing of limitations, exemplified by the apostle Paul's discussion of his "thorn in the flesh" in 2 Corinthians 12. Paul believed that this thorn had become the vessel by which God gave him grace and strength. It wasn't Paul's freedoms and abilities that made him what he was. Instead, his weakness, his limitations made him what he was.

I didn't teach this specifically with Anthony in mind. In fact, had I thought beforehand that the sermon would so closely parallel Anthony's troubles, I probably would have been concerned the whole time that I might be perceived as publicly singling him out. For better or worse, if I had prepared the sermon with him in mind, I undoubtedly would have taught on something else. But the ignorance allowed me to simply teach the text without fear of impropriety.

At the conclusion, we had an altar call. After everyone else had left the altar, Anthony was still there kneeling at the platform steps. I winced. With great trepidation I now realized what had been done, and while I prayed with him, I couldn't help but mentally play over in my mind what I had said and how it must have sounded to him and his family. I hoped to God I hadn't trivialized his suffering.

A week later Anthony approached and, to my relief, thanked me for the message. He then told me that he had been afraid of being thought of only as (in his words) "the guy with cancer." He had feared that he would be defined by cancer instead of by his actual work, that cancer would lower the bar and put an asterisk next to his ministry. "Yeah," Anthony said, imagining someone in the future evaluating his ministry, "that's a good song or a good sermon, especially considering he had cancer." But he said that the message had helped him see his cancer as an inseparable part of his life and ministry. It was, he concluded, the channel by which God's grace was pouring into his life.

While he was speaking, I realized that one week earlier I had, in a way, been praying at the altar with Paul's own gospel-son. At that very altar had knelt the one living man I knew who most exemplified what Paul taught in 2 Corinthians 12: that Christ's strength is made *perfect* in weakness.

I heard music—biblical teaching set to the music of Anthony's life. I understood grace more deeply—grace as it was meant to be understood, not as a word on a page or even merely as a synonym for forgiveness but as that which transfigures the very ugliest things, the most hopeless things, like a cross, turning them into a strength that saves.

THE SUIT AND TIE

The second moment that stands out occurred one Sunday morning in the last few months of Anthony's life. I had left the service momentarily and went out into the parking lot to get something out of my car. On my way back in I saw his car. His wife, Lysandra, was in the driver's seat, and Anthony was in the passenger's seat, slumped over while Lysandra was trying to comfort him. I remember wanting to go over to the car to see if I could help, but an internal warning whispered that this was a deeply private moment, so I resisted the impulse and went back inside the sanctuary. But the image stayed with me. Anthony was wearing his suit and tie, ready for church, but his body had so completely abandoned him that he didn't have the strength to sit up straight, much less go into the service. But the suit and tie. The suit. And tie.

This was his life. The pediment I mentioned earlier comes to mind again. Dressed and ready for service—a service into which he could not go. If anyone had an excuse to just show up in whatever state he could muster, it was Anthony. But he didn't. He tried to look his best. Jesus once said,

> *"Moreover, when you fast, do not be like the hypocrites, with a sad countenance. For they disfigure their faces that they may appear to men to be fasting. . . .*
> *But you, when you fast, anoint your head and wash your face, so that you do not appear to men to be fasting, but to your Father who is in the secret place; and your Father who sees in secret will reward you openly."*
> (Matthew 6:16–18 NKJV)

When I remembered this verse later, I knew why I had been warned not to approach the car. It seems Anthony didn't want to enter the service and be seen with a fallen countenance and extreme weakness; he didn't want to put on a show of suffering. This was for the heavenly Father's eyes alone. For us, if we were to see him at all, he was determined to be seen in a suit and tie, his face washed, as it were, and his head anointed with oil.

NO ONE GREATER

The third and final defining moment for me occurred not in Anthony's life but in his death. At his funeral was played the video of him and his fellow vocalists singing "None like Our God." I had heard this song many times before, but it was a very different song now. It had taken on a quality that I can describe only as sublime. The term *sublime* was originally conceived as a word to describe that peculiar feeling of awe and holy terror, the sense that something from beyond this world was in the next room. It haunted me—the face of Anthony on the screen overhead and the face of Anthony below in the casket, dressed in a suit and tie. He was singing in the video; and, unsummoned, the words of Hebrews rolled in tickertape across my mind: "By faith Abel offered to God a more excellent sacrifice . . . and through [faith] he being dead still speaks" (Hebrews 11:4 NKJV).

I had always marveled at the faith expressed in Anthony's song. He had been in the grip of cancer and had sung the song in faith. But now, while his body lay in the casket, the song sounded different. When a bird sings in a forest of maple trees, the wood from the maples, like the wood in a guitar, reverberates with the sound and produces a highly resonant acoustic timbre. It's a sound that can be heard only in such a forest.

Just so, the sound of Anthony's song was coming from somewhere else. It was rich with the timbre of heaven. He was now standing at the center, the very fount of all being, his eyes beholding the glory that the apostle John saw and wrote about. Thunder was emanating from under the throne of God. Anthony was on the other side of eternity now, declaring for us who live in the shadowlands of this world, "I have now seen him, and there is none like our God."

The song, like a hundred velvet hammers, fell on my face:

Mighty Savior, my strong tower
No one greater, no one greater
Mountain mover, my defender
No one greater, no one greater[20]

These words were now sung by one who surveyed the throne. This was almost too much for my mortal flesh. To maintain my composure, I closed my eyes. A few minutes later, when I thought I was back in control, I opened them. The overhead screens were dark. We weren't watching video anymore. Anthony's part in the song had ended, but not the song itself. The same vocalists who had been singing in the video were now standing on the platform and had picked up the song seamlessly. A congregation of more than 500 voices—now breathing some of the same heavenly

---

20. "Like Our God" (Weldon Music Publishing, 2016).

air Anthony was breathing—sang, *No one greater, no one greater.* A baton had been handed off. We were being led by a conductor who had graduated to the very presence of God. Anthony's voice became the voice of many.

CONCLUSION

I had entered the service, seen the casket, and found myself unwillingly in awe of death and the way in which it had claimed someone so young and so good. But then the song had begun: "There's an anthem rising from the ashes." By the time we finished singing Anthony's song, everything was the other way around. I had heard an anthem in the truest sense of the word. Indeed, if death had thought to silence Anthony's voice, it was sorely mistaken. Death had never seemed more powerless, more obsolete. Cancer had put Anthony in the casket, but in doing so it had handed him a megaphone. I understood better now what grace would sound like if it were a song. That song was Anthony himself, a song made perfect in weakness.

LIVE LIKE ANTHONY

- What is your favorite song written by Anthony? What do the words of that song speak to you?

- What is your favorite scriptural psalm? What do the words of that psalm speak to you?

- Take an entire day and listen to Anthony Trimble's music and let the words and the worship inspire you to live like Anthony.

AFTERWORD

Michael Ensey

I hope through this book you have come to know Anthony better and have gained some insight into the character of a man who moved heaven and touched earth in less than thirty-six years. Following are some closing observations about Anthony that I'm sure you would be quick to discern yourself if you were having coffee with him. I trust that the life lessons he taught will challenge all of us to be better and do more with our own lives.

ASK GOOD QUESTIONS

Anthony was such a great teacher because he was such a great student of life. He studied the Word of God. He studied people. He studied great leaders and processes and systems and best practices. You can discern a lot about the character and intelligence of someone not just by the content of the person's answers but also by the quality of his or her questions. Anthony asked good questions. He was always seeking to learn, to grow, to be better, and to do more for the kingdom of God. Anthony taught us how to ask good questions.

PURSUE EXCELLENCE

In a previous chapter I mentioned visiting with Anthony in a hotel room just a few days before he passed away. I had preached at Restoration Church earlier that day. He wasn't feeling good enough to attend the service, but he did watch online. And in the midst of all the really serious things we were discussing, somehow that conversation always made its way back to talking about church. He was asking questions: "What did you think about the service format?" "What are your thoughts about our platform arrangement?" "What can we do better?" "How can we be more effective?" "Can you ask my dad to speed up the preliminaries a little?" He passionately pursued excellence, always striving to increase his capacity and fulfill his potential. He was a team builder and made everyone around him better. Whether in the local church, district youth ministry, or on a national stage, Anthony taught us how to pursue excellence.

CHOOSE JOY

Anthony lived life with a certain joy. He had a radiant smile and was quick to show it. And he had a quirky sense of humor, even to the very end. In his last few days in a sweet and solemn moment, the family was singing a slow, somber song about the peace of God when all of a sudden Anthony broke into a gospel song with a thumping beat about God being more than enough! Anthony absolutely believed that! It was startling to hear him profess that kind of loud faith in that quiet moment! Anthony taught us how to live life more abundantly and with overflowing joy even in the darkest of days.

BE A CHRISTIAN

While Anthony was a powerful preacher and an anointed musician, singer, and songwriter, he was an even better Christian. It is reported that the late great preacher and leader Reverend J. T. Pugh once said, "It's always good when a preacher is a Christian." I concur. And Anthony was truly a Christian. He was the most genuine person I've ever met. He was pure in heart and pure in spirit. Jesus said, "Blessed are the pure in heart, for they shall see God" (Matthew 5:8 NKJV). He had that kind of heart—and now he has experienced the fulfillment of that promise. He taught us how to be Christians.

LOVE PEOPLE

Anthony was such a great person in so many ways and in so many different spheres of life. He was blessed with a variety of different talents, many of which were visible on the stage as he sang and preached. However, I think his greatest talents were probably more subtle. One of those was his relational ability. He was so genuine in his approach to people. He knew how to establish, develop, and maintain healthy relationships with the right people. Each person who wrote a chapter in this book had a very close personal relationship with Anthony. That required a special ability, and Anthony had it. He loved ministry, but there was nothing more important to Anthony than his family. His ministry started at home and extended outward from there. He took each role seriously as a son, brother, husband, and especially as a father. Anthony taught us how to love people and how to care for our families.

TRUST GOD

We are writing this book because our expectations did not intersect with God's purpose or his performance. We prayed and believed for a different outcome, but there is such a great chasm between his ways and our ways, between his thoughts and our thoughts. That's why we don't lean on our own understanding—it's so insufficient. Trust wasn't made for good times when we have all the answers and the way forward is clear. Trust is necessary when our world is shattered—when we sit in darkness. We trust when we do not understand. So in all of our ways, when we have no answers and we have no words, just the acknowledgment of the reality of our God is enough. We acknowledge him, and he directs our paths. (See Proverbs 3:5–6.)

I believe the prophet Isaiah was trying to help someone who was wrestling with the untimely loss of a loved one when he penned these words:

> *Good people pass away; the godly often*
> *die before their time. . . . God is protecting them*
> *from the evil to come. For those who follow godly*
> *paths will rest in peace when they die.*
> (Isaiah 57:1–2 NLT)

It is into that great chasm of grief that God inserts his sufficient grace. When God says no, his grace fills the void of our disappointment and unmet expectations. Anthony taught us to trust God. Always.

OBEY THE GOSPEL

We continue grieving the loss of our friend, and that's okay. It is normal. It is natural. When we love deeply, we hurt deeply. But we do not sorrow as those who have no hope. Anthony prepared for this day, and he prepared well. Like Job, he came face to face with death and never blinked. "Though he slay me, yet will I trust in him" (Job 13:15). "The Lord gave, and the Lord hath taketh away; blessed be the name of the Lord" (Job 1:21). Like the apostle Paul living life on the edge of time and eternity, Anthony gave his all, leaving no margin for unfulfilled potential.

Anthony prepared for the day of his departure from this life by obeying the gospel of Jesus Christ—his death, burial, and resurrection. He repented of his sins, was buried with Christ in water baptism in the name of Jesus, and received the baptism of the Holy Ghost with the initial sign of speaking in other tongues as the Spirit of God gave the ability. (See John 3:3–5; Acts 2:1–4, 38.) He loved the new-birth message. He believed it. He lived it. He preached it. He wrote songs about it. It is that same message that continues to give us hope today.

The perfect sinless sacrifice of Jesus Christ on the cross reversed the curse of sin. The penalty of sin is death, but through the power of the gospel the law of the Spirit of life in Christ Jesus has made us free from the law of sin and death. (See Romans 8:2.) Through the power of the cross Jesus took the penalty of sin, which is death, and turned it into our entrance into eternal life. He turned the penalty into a promise.

That's why the death of one of his saints is so precious to God; it is a reminder of his greatest victory on the cross. "O death, where is thy sting? O grave, where is thy victory? The sting of death is sin; and the strength of sin is the law. But thanks be to God, which giveth us the victory through our Lord Jesus Christ" (1 Corinthians 15:55–57). Death is no longer punishment—it is our entrance into glory. Anthony taught us how to prepare for eternity by obeying the gospel.

CONCLUSION

As Anthony took his last breath in this life and for the first time took a deep, pure, pain-free breath in the next life, I have a feeling he crossed that finish line and announced his arrival by saying, "I'm here! I'm here to worship! Ain't no rock gonna take my place. I'm here to worship!"[11] If we're going to live like Anthony is living right now in eternity, then we are going to have to live as he lived while he was here on earth—holding loosely to this life and reaching for the invisible eternal world.

Just a few days before Anthony transitioned from this life, he wrote a song titled "Dream of Heaven." He knew he was close to finishing his course and receiving his reward. And now we're dreaming of joining him there.

There's a place where we'll never get old
Where the streets have been paved with gold
As you gently fall asleep dream of heaven
Dream of heaven

---

11. "Like Our God" (Weldon Music Publishing, 2016).

There's a place where we'll dance with the stars
Where we'll be not as we are
As you gently fall asleep dream of heaven
Dream of heaven

Oh, oh, oh
Oh, oh, oh
Dream of heaven and the place it will be
Dream of heaven and the possibilities

One day soon we'll see His face
Surrounded by the most amazing grace
You can hear the angels sing
As you dream of heaven
Won't you dream of heaven

Oh, oh, oh
Oh, oh, oh
Dream of heaven and the place it will be
Dream of heaven and the possibilities[12]

---

12. "Dream of Heaven" (Weldon Music Publishing, 2023).

APPENDIX

SUPPORT FOR ANTHONY'S FAMILY

Please use the information provided below if you would like to send financial support directly to Anthony's family.

Cash App: $LiveLikeAnthony
Checks: Payable to Lysandra Trimble
    Restoration Church
    Attn: Lysandra Trimble
    1040 Fairgrounds Rd.
    St. Charles, MO 63301

ANTHONY TRIMBLE MEDIA

Purchase and listen to Anthony Trimble's music via—
    Apple Music: Anthony Trimble
    Amazon Music: Anthony Trimble
    www.YouTube.com: Anthony Trimble Music

View Anthony Trimble's preaching via—
    www.YouTube.com: Anthony Trimble Preaching

All proceeds from the sale of this book will be used to support missions and ministry in the name of Anthony Trimble.